Park and Play

Discovering National Parks from the Comfort of Your RV

Sarah Miller

Table of Contents

INTRODUCTION **6**

CHAPTER I: The National Park System **8**

A brief history of the National Park System 8

The significance of preserving natural and cultural treasures 11

How national parks are managed and maintained 14

The diversity of national parks across the United States 17

CHAPTER II: Choosing Your RV **21**

The different types of RVs available 21

Factors to consider when selecting an RV 23

Budgeting for your RV adventure 26

Tips for buying or renting the right RV for your needs . 29

CHAPTER III: Preparing for the Journey **33**

Planning your national park road trip 33

Creating a travel itinerary 36

Packing essentials for RV travel 39

Safety and maintenance checks before hitting the road 42

CHAPTER IV: Hitting the Road **46**

Tips for navigating RV-friendly routes 46

The RV lifestyle: What to expect on the road 49

Managing your travel budget 51

Finding RV-friendly campsites and accommodations ... 54

CHAPTER V: Exploring National Parks 58

Highlights from some of the most popular national parks
.... 58

Lesser-known gems worth exploring 61

Activities and attractions within the parks 63

Wildlife encounters and safety precautions 66

CHAPTER VI: Making the Most of Your Visit 70

Tips for avoiding crowds 70

Capturing memories with photography 73

Connecting with fellow RV travelers 75

Planning for unexpected challenges 78

CHAPTER VII: Going Green on the Road 81

Sustainable RV travel practices 81

Reducing your environmental footprint 84

Responsible camping and waste disposal 86

Supporting conservation efforts within national parks . 89

CHAPTER VIII: The RV Lifestyle and Community 93

The sense of community among RV travelers 93

Personal stories and experiences from RV enthusiasts 95

RV clubs and organizations 98

How the RV lifestyle can enrich your life..................... 101

CHAPTER IX: Returning Home and Reflection 105

Dealing with post-trip blues 105

The lasting impact of national park exploration 108

Planning your next RV adventure 111

Final thoughts and encouragement to continue exploring 114

CONCLUSION 118

INTRODUCTION

Welcome to a journey of adventure, natural wonder, and the freedom of the open road! In "Park and Play: Discovering National Parks from the Comfort of Your RV," we invite you to explore some of the most magnificent landscapes and cultural treasures the United States has to offer.

The allure of national parks has captivated the hearts of travelers for generations. From the majestic peaks of the Rocky Mountains to the dramatic canyons of the Southwest, from the lush forests of the Pacific Northwest to the historic sites of the East Coast, our national parks represent a tapestry of unparalleled beauty and heritage. These protected spaces serve as living classrooms in ecology, geology, history, and so much more, offering endless opportunities for adventure and discovery.

In recent years, there has been a resurgence in the love for road travel, particularly in the form of recreational vehicles (RVs). The freedom to wander where you please, the comfort of your own rolling home, and the chance to wake up amidst the natural beauty of national parks are just a few of the reasons why RV travel has become a beloved American pastime.

This book is your guide to combining these passions— exploring the national parks while enjoying the comfort and convenience of RV travel. Whether you're an RV enthusiast looking for new destinations or a national park lover interested in experiencing these treasures in a new way, "Park and Play" is your essential companion. In the following chapters, we'll provide you with everything you need to know to plan, prepare, and embark on the journey of a lifetime, discovering the wonders of our national parks from the comfort of your RV. So, let's hit the road and begin our adventure together!

CHAPTER I

The National Park System

A brief history of the National Park System

The story of the National Park System in the United States is one of foresight, preservation, and an enduring commitment to safeguarding the nation's most precious natural and cultural treasures. Born out of recognizing the need to protect these pristine landscapes for future generations, the National Park System has grown from humble beginnings to become a cornerstone of American conservation and outdoor recreation.

The origins of the National Park System can be traced back to the mid-19th century, a time when industrialization and westward expansion were rapidly transforming the American landscape. As settlers pushed westward, there was growing concern that the country's unique and breathtaking natural wonders were at risk of being lost forever. In this context, the idea of preserving these areas for their scenic and scientific value first began to take root.

One of the earliest catalysts for establishing the National Park System was the publication of "The Yosemite Book" by Thomas Starr King in 1868. King's vivid descriptions of the Yosemite Valley in California stirred public interest and inspired advocates for its protection. Two years later, President Abraham Lincoln signed the Yosemite Grant Act into law, granting the Yosemite Valley and the Mariposa Grove of Giant Sequoias to the state of California to preserve these natural wonders.

The establishment of Yellowstone National Park in 1872 marked a pivotal moment in the history of conservation worldwide. Located in what is now Wyoming, Montana, and Idaho, Yellowstone became the world's first national park, setting a precedent for protecting and preserving natural landscapes. This momentous step was driven by the visionary leadership of individuals like Ferdinand Hayden and George Bird Grinnell, who recognized the importance of preserving Yellowstone's unique geothermal wonders, abundant wildlife, and pristine wilderness for future generations. President Ulysses S. Grant signed the legislation into law, cementing the concept of national parks in the American consciousness.

Following the success of Yellowstone, the United States continued to expand its national park system, with the creation of Mackinac National Park in Michigan in 1875 and Sequoia and Yosemite National Parks in California in 1890. The latter marked a significant milestone as it established the federal government's role in managing and protecting national parks, a role that would later be formalized with the passage of the National Park Service Organic Act in 1916.

The National Park Service Organic Act, signed into law by President Woodrow Wilson, marked the birth of the National Park Service (NPS) as a federal agency responsible for the administration and oversight of national parks. Stephen Mather, the first director of the NPS, played a pivotal role in shaping the agency's mission and vision. Under his leadership, the NPS adopted a unified system of management, prioritized visitor services, and worked tirelessly to expand the national park system. The NPS quickly added parks such as Acadia, Grand Canyon, and Zion to its roster, preserving a diverse array of natural landscapes for the enjoyment and education of the American people.

The expansion of the National Park System was not limited to natural wonders. Recognizing the need to protect America's cultural heritage, Congress passed the Antiquities Act in 1906, granting the President the authority to designate national monuments. Presidents like Theodore Roosevelt and Woodrow Wilson used this legislation to protect historic sites and cultural landmarks. In 1916, President Wilson signed the legislation that formally established the National Park Service, giving it the mission to "conserve the scenery and the natural and historic objects and the wild life therein and to provide for the enjoyment of the same in such manner and by such means as will leave them unimpaired for the enjoyment of future generations."

Throughout the 20th century, the National Park System continued to expand, adding iconic parks such as the Great Smoky Mountains, Everglades, and Denali. The system evolved to include various sites, from battlefields and historic homes to seashores and recreation areas. The preservation and interpretation of these sites became central to the NPS's mission, ensuring that both natural and cultural heritage were protected and shared with the public.

Today, the National Park System boasts over 400 units, each with its own unique story and significance. These sites collectively reflect the rich tapestry of America's natural beauty, history, and culture. The National Park System is a testament to the foresight and dedication of those who recognized the importance of preserving these treasures for the benefit of present and future generations. It stands as a symbol of America's commitment to conservation, education, and the enduring value of our natural and cultural heritage. As we continue to explore and cherish these national treasures, we ensure that the legacy of the National Park System endures for centuries to come.

The significance of preserving natural and cultural treasures

The preservation of natural and cultural treasures holds a profound significance that extends far beyond mere conservation efforts. It encompasses recognizing the intrinsic value of our planet's diverse ecosystems, geographies, and species, as well as preserving humanity's collective heritage. In the face of environmental degradation, urbanization, and rapid development, the importance of safeguarding these treasures becomes increasingly apparent. This section explores the multifaceted significance of preserving natural and cultural treasures, delving into this imperative endeavor's intrinsic, ecological, educational, and societal dimensions.

At its core, preserving natural and cultural treasures acknowledges the intrinsic value of the world's wonders. Natural wonders, from the towering peaks of the Himalayas to the intricate ecosystems of coral reefs, possess a beauty and complexity that transcends human utility. Their existence is a testament to the magnificence of the natural world and our interconnectedness with it. Similarly, cultural treasures, such as ancient temples, historic landmarks, and artistic masterpieces, are manifestations of human creativity, innovation, and the rich tapestry of our shared history. These creations reflect the depth of human expression and serve as a source of inspiration and reflection for future generations. Preserving these treasures is an affirmation of their worth in and of themselves, independent of any practical or utilitarian value they may hold.

From an ecological perspective, preserving natural treasures is pivotal in maintaining the delicate balance of our planet's ecosystems. Biodiversity, for instance, is a cornerstone of ecological stability. Each species plays a unique role in its ecosystem, no matter how small or seemingly insignificant. The loss of even a single species can disrupt the intricate web of interactions that sustains life on Earth. Preserving natural habitats ensures that ecosystems remain resilient, capable of adapting to environmental changes and supporting a diverse array of life forms. Additionally, natural treasures often serve as vital refuges for endangered species, offering protection and sanctuary in an increasingly fragmented and human-dominated world. By safeguarding these areas, we safeguard the survival of countless species and the planet's health.

Cultural treasures, too, hold ecological significance. Indigenous knowledge and traditional practices often incorporate a deep understanding of local ecosystems and sustainable resource management. The preservation of cultural heritage not only respects the wisdom of these practices but can also provide valuable insights for modern conservation efforts. Furthermore, the very act of preserving cultural sites and traditions fosters a sense of connection and stewardship towards the environment, reinforcing the importance of caring for the natural world. Education is another vital dimension of preserving natural and cultural treasures. These treasures serve as living classrooms, offering opportunities for learning, inspiration, and personal growth. Natural wonders provide insights into the Earth's geological and ecological processes, fostering scientific curiosity and environmental awareness. Experiencing the magnificence of landscapes like the Grand Canyon or the Serengeti can ignite a passion for conservation and a sense of responsibility for the planet's well-being. Similarly, cultural treasures provide windows into humanity's diverse cultures, histories, and artistic expressions. They offer a profound appreciation for the achievements and struggles of previous generations and help us understand our place in the continuum of human history. Preserving these treasures ensures that future generations have access to these invaluable educational resources, empowering them to learn, explore, and connect with the world around them.

Beyond their educational value, preserving natural and cultural treasures also has significant societal implications. It fosters a sense of identity, pride, and unity among communities and nations. Cultural landmarks and traditions are woven into the fabric of societies, serving as symbols of heritage and continuity. Preserving these elements is essential for maintaining cultural diversity and resilience in the face of globalization. Similarly, natural treasures often hold deep cultural and spiritual significance for indigenous communities, connecting them to their ancestral lands and traditions. Recognizing and respecting these connections is essential for fostering social equity and environmental justice.

Furthermore, the preservation of these treasures has economic benefits. Natural wonders and cultural landmarks often serve as magnets for tourism, attracting visitors from around the world. The revenue generated from tourism can support local economies, create jobs, and fund conservation efforts. Additionally, the preservation of these treasures contributes to the overall quality of life by providing recreational opportunities, green spaces, and cultural enrichment. It enhances the well-being of communities and individuals alike, making it an essential component of sustainable development.

In conclusion, the significance of preserving natural and cultural treasures transcends the boundaries of ecology, education, and society. It encompasses the recognition of intrinsic value, ecological stability, educational enrichment, and societal well-being. As stewards of this planet and its rich cultural heritage, we are responsible for protecting and preserving these treasures for ourselves and future generations. In doing so, we honor our world's remarkable beauty, diversity, and complexity and ensure that it continues to inspire, educate, and sustain us in the years ahead.

How national parks are managed and maintained

National parks are not merely pieces of land set aside for public enjoyment; they are carefully managed and maintained to ensure their preservation and protection. The National Park Service (NPS), a federal agency established in 1916, is responsible for managing and maintaining these natural and cultural treasures. Managing national parks is a complex and multifaceted endeavor, encompassing various aspects, including resource protection, visitor services, education, and infrastructure maintenance. This section explores how national parks are managed and maintained, shedding light on the intricate balance between conservation and recreation that characterizes these iconic landscapes.

At the heart of national park management is the commitment to preserving the natural and cultural resources within park boundaries. This involves a range of scientific and ecological practices to protect the integrity of ecosystems, species, and historical sites. The NPS conducts extensive research to monitor and understand the health of park ecosystems. This research informs conservation strategies, such as habitat restoration, invasive species control, and wildlife management. The goal is to maintain the ecological balance and biodiversity that defines these areas, ensuring that future generations can experience the same natural wonders that have captivated visitors for decades.

Resource protection extends to cultural heritage as well. National parks often contain historic buildings, archaeological sites, and cultural artifacts that provide insights into the nation's history and diverse cultures. The NPS works diligently to preserve these treasures through careful restoration, documentation, and education. Park rangers and cultural resource specialists are crucial in managing and maintaining cultural sites, ensuring they remain accessible and intact for visitors while respecting their historical and cultural significance.

Visitor services are another integral component of national park management. National parks welcome millions of visitors annually, and providing for their safety, education, and enjoyment is paramount. Park rangers serve as ambassadors and educators, offering guided tours, educational programs, and interpretive materials to enhance the visitor experience. Additionally, visitor centers, campgrounds, and hiking trails are meticulously maintained to ensure accessibility and safety. The NPS strives to balance offering recreational opportunities and minimizing the impact of human presence on the natural environment.

Education is a central pillar of national park management. Parks aim to inspire visitors and foster a deeper understanding of the natural world and cultural heritage. Interpretive programs, exhibits, and publications are designed to engage visitors with each park's unique stories and values. Through education, visitors gain a greater appreciation for the importance of conservation and preservation, encouraging a sense of stewardship toward these cherished places. National parks also collaborate with schools and communities to extend their educational reach, ensuring that a broad and diverse audience appreciates their value.

Infrastructure maintenance is an often-unseen but crucial aspect of managing national parks. Roads, bridges, visitor centers, and utility systems require regular upkeep to ensure the safety and convenience of visitors. The NPS invests significant resources in infrastructure maintenance and improvement, addressing issues such as erosion, water quality, and accessibility. Modernizing and maintaining park infrastructure enhances the visitor experience and supports the long-term preservation of these landscapes.

Furthermore, the NPS places a strong emphasis on sustainability and environmental stewardship. National parks serve as models for eco-friendly practices, from energy-efficient buildings and renewable energy sources to waste reduction and water conservation initiatives. These efforts reduce the parks' environmental footprint and inspire visitors to adopt sustainable practices in their own lives.

Volunteerism and partnerships are essential components of national park management. Many national parks rely on the support of dedicated volunteers and collaborative efforts with nonprofit organizations and local communities. Volunteers contribute their time and expertise to various activities, including trail maintenance, wildlife monitoring, and educational programs. Partnerships with conservation groups and local businesses help fund critical projects and engage the broader community in preserving these natural and cultural treasures.

The financing of national park management and maintenance is a complex issue. While the NPS receives federal funding, it often falls short of meeting the needs of the growing park system. Entrance fees, donations, and revenue from concessions also play a significant role in supporting park operations. However, the funding gap remains challenging, leading to deferred maintenance and infrastructure needs that require creative solutions and advocacy efforts.

In conclusion, managing and maintaining national parks is a multifaceted and dynamic undertaking. Balancing the preservation of natural and cultural treasures with the provision of visitor services and education requires careful planning, research, and dedication. The National Park Service, along with volunteers, partners, and communities, works tirelessly to ensure that these iconic landscapes continue to inspire, educate, and provide solace for future generations. National parks stand as testaments to the value of conservation and the enduring legacy of our nation's commitment to preserving its most precious natural and cultural treasures.

The diversity of national parks across the United States

The United States is a country renowned for its remarkable diversity, and nowhere is this more evident than in its national parks. From the rugged coasts of Acadia in Maine to the volcanic landscapes of Hawai'i Volcanoes in the Pacific, and from the sweeping vistas of the Grand Canyon in Arizona to the lush forests of Great Smoky Mountains on the border of North Carolina and Tennessee, the nation's national parks offer an astonishing array of natural and cultural wonders. This section explores the incredible diversity of national parks across the United States, highlighting the unique features, landscapes, and experiences that make each one a distinct and cherished treasure.

One of the most striking aspects of the national parks in the United States is the sheer geographical diversity they encompass. Consider the juxtaposition of Alaska's Denali National Park, home to the continent's highest peak, Denali (formerly known as Mount McKinley), and Florida's Everglades National Park, a vast expanse of wetlands and subtropical wilderness. These two parks represent the extreme ends of the country's climatic and topographic spectrum, offering visitors vastly different experiences. Denali's rugged terrain is a haven for mountaineers, wildlife enthusiasts, and those seeking solitude amid pristine wilderness, while the Everglades provide a haven for birdwatchers, boaters, and those interested in exploring the unique ecosystem of this "river of grass."

Similarly, the diversity of national parks extends to their geological features. Arches National Park in Utah showcases a surreal landscape of red rock arches, pinnacles, and fins, sculpted by millions of years of erosion. In contrast, the watery wonderland of Voyageurs National Park in Minnesota is defined by its interconnected network of lakes, islands, and waterways, perfect for canoeing, fishing, and stargazing. These parks exemplify the geologic diversity of the United States, with each one telling a story of Earth's dynamic processes and history.

Cultural diversity is also a hallmark of the national parks. Mesa Verde National Park in Colorado preserves the ancient cliff dwellings and artifacts of the Ancestral Puebloans, providing a glimpse into the rich Native American history of the region. Meanwhile, the Statue of Liberty National Monument in New York Harbor symbolizes freedom and immigration, welcoming newcomers to the United States for over a century. The array of cultural sites within national parks reflects the tapestry of American history and the nation's commitment to preserving its heritage.

Biodiversity is yet another facet of the diversity found in national parks. Great Smoky Mountains National Park, a UNESCO World Heritage Site, is renowned for its remarkable biological diversity, housing an estimated 19,000 documented species, including a rich diversity of plant life. Olympic National Park in Washington State encompasses everything from temperate rainforests to rugged coastline, providing habitats for diverse wildlife, from Roosevelt elk to bald eagles. The parks' commitment to protecting and preserving these ecosystems ensures that future generations can continue to marvel at the variety of life forms found within their boundaries.

The architectural diversity of national parks is also noteworthy. While many parks embrace a rustic aesthetic, such as the historic lodges of Yellowstone or the stone towers of Bryce Canyon, others feature distinctive architectural styles that reflect the cultural and historical context of the region. The Southwestern-inspired structures in Chaco Culture National Historical Park in New Mexico or the Art Deco design of Hoover Dam, which impounds Lake Mead, are prime examples. These architectural gems not only enhance the visitor experience but also serve as reminders of the human presence in these landscapes throughout history.

Accessibility and recreational diversity are vital aspects of national parks as well. While some parks, like Yosemite in California, offer world-class rock climbing, others, such as Mammoth Cave in Kentucky, beckon explorers into subterranean worlds of underground chambers and passageways. Accessibility features ensure that people of all abilities can enjoy the parks, with designated trails, visitor centers, and interpretive programs designed to accommodate diverse needs. Whether it's hiking, camping, birdwatching, or simply gazing at the night sky, there's something for everyone in national parks across the country.

The national parks' role in preserving and protecting marine environments should not be overlooked. Dry Tortugas National Park in Florida, for instance, protects a remote cluster of islands and coral reefs, providing a haven for marine life and world-class snorkeling opportunities. Similarly, Channel Islands National Park in California encompasses five rugged islands and their surrounding waters, serving as a refuge for rare species and a living laboratory for scientific research. These marine sanctuaries offer visitors a chance to explore the wonders of the underwater world, adding yet another layer to the diversity of experiences found within the national park system.

In conclusion, the diversity of national parks across the United States is a testament to the nation's rich natural and cultural heritage. From the Arctic tundra of Gates of the Arctic National Park in Alaska to the tropical paradise of the Virgin Islands National Park in the Caribbean, each park offers a unique window into the beauty and complexity of the world we inhabit. These protected landscapes and cultural sites reflect the nation's commitment to preservation, conservation, and the enduring value of these treasured places. As visitors explore the diversity of national parks, they gain not only a deeper understanding of the country's natural and cultural heritage but also an appreciation for the boundless wonders that make the United States a land of unparalleled diversity and beauty.

CHAPTER II

Choosing Your RV

The different types of RVs available

Recreational vehicles (RVs) have become synonymous with the spirit of adventure and the freedom of the open road. These versatile vehicles offer a home on wheels, allowing travelers to explore the world with all the comforts and conveniences of home. The world of RVs is incredibly diverse, with various options to suit various preferences and needs. From compact camper vans to luxurious motorhomes, this section explores the different types of RVs available, each offering a unique way to experience the joy of RV travel.

Camper vans, also known as Class B motorhomes, are the smallest and most compact of all RV types. Built on van chassis, these vehicles are easy to maneuver and park, making them ideal for solo travelers or couples. They typically feature a small kitchenette, a sleeping area, and a compact bathroom. Camper vans balance mobility and comfort, providing a cozy and self-contained living space for those looking to explore on a smaller scale.

Travel trailers are popular among RV enthusiasts for their affordability and versatility. These trailers are towed behind a vehicle, allowing travelers to detach and explore their destination without needing a separate motorhome. Travel trailers come in various sizes and layouts, from compact teardrop trailers to spacious models with multiple slide-outs. They offer a range of amenities, including kitchens, bathrooms, and sleeping quarters, making them suitable for families and groups of all sizes.

Fifth-wheel trailers are a subtype of travel trailers but feature a unique hitch design that connects to a pickup truck's bed rather than a traditional hitch at the rear of a towing vehicle. This design offers increased stability and maneuverability, making them a preferred choice for larger RVs. Fifth-wheel trailers often have multiple slide-outs, providing generous living spaces, fully-equipped kitchens, and spacious bedrooms. These RVs are well-suited for extended stays and full-time RV living.

Toy haulers combine the features of a travel trailer or fifth-wheel with a dedicated garage space in the rear for storing recreational vehicles, such as motorcycles, ATVs, or bicycles. This versatility allows outdoor enthusiasts to bring their toys along for the adventure. The garage area can also be converted into additional living space, making toy haulers an excellent choice for those who want both adventure and comfort on the road.

Class C motorhomes are characterized by their distinctive cab-over design, with a bed or additional storage space located above the driver's cab. These RVs are built on van or truck chassis and are known for their convenience and user-friendly features. They typically offer a kitchen, bathroom, sleeping quarters, and ample storage. Class C motorhomes are popular for families due to their comfortable layouts and ability to sleep multiple people.

Class A motorhomes are the largest and most luxurious RVs on the market. These behemoths often resemble buses and offer spacious interiors with all the desired amenities. They are built on custom chassis and can range from 25 to 45 feet long. Class A motorhomes feature full kitchens, bathrooms, entertainment systems, and plenty of storage. Some even have luxurious features like king-sized beds, washer/dryer units, and multiple slide-outs. These RVs provide a true home-away-from-home experience and are favored by those seeking comfort and style.

Truck campers are compact and lightweight RVs that fit into the bed of a pickup truck. They offer a minimalist approach to RV living, typically featuring a small kitchenette, sleeping area, and basic bathroom facilities. Truck campers are highly maneuverable and well-suited for off-road adventures. Their affordability and versatility make them an excellent choice for solo travelers and outdoor enthusiasts who want to explore remote areas.

Pop-up campers, also known as tent trailers or folding campers, are compact and lightweight towable RVs. When in transit, they have a low-profile design, but when parked, they can be expanded to reveal a pop-up top, creating additional headroom and sleeping space. Pop-up campers offer basic amenities, including sleeping areas, a small kitchenette, and sometimes a bathroom. They are an excellent option for budget-conscious campers who want a more comfortable alternative to traditional tent camping.

In conclusion, the world of RVs is as diverse as the landscapes they allow travelers to explore. The different types of RVs available cater to various preferences, budgets, and travel styles. Whether you're a solo adventurer seeking simplicity or a family looking for a spacious home on wheels, there's an RV type to suit your needs. Each type offers a unique blend of mobility, comfort, and convenience, ensuring that RV enthusiasts can find the perfect vehicle to embark on their own road to adventure.

Factors to consider when selecting an RV

Choosing the right recreational vehicle (RV) is a pivotal decision for those who seek the freedom of the open road and the adventure of RV travel. RVs come in various shapes, sizes, and configurations, each tailored to different needs and preferences. Selecting the perfect RV involves carefully considering several factors, from the type of RV that suits your travel style to your budget and specific requirements.

The first and foremost decision in selecting an RV is determining the type that best fits your needs. Consider the various types available, such as camper vans, travel trailers, fifth-wheel trailers, Class C motorhomes, Class A motorhomes, truck campers, and pop-up campers. Each type offers a unique combination of size, amenities, and mobility. For example, a camper van might be ideal if you prefer a compact and agile option for solo travel or a couple's getaway. Conversely, large families or those seeking luxury and space may lean towards Class A motorhomes or spacious fifth-wheel trailers.

Define the primary purpose and intended use of your RV. Are you planning short weekend getaways, extended road trips, or full-time RV living? Your usage patterns will influence the type of RV and the features you require. Those planning long-term travel may prioritize amenities like a full kitchen, comfortable sleeping arrangements, and ample storage space. Weekend warriors may be content with a simpler setup and focus more on mobility and ease of setup.

The size and layout of an RV play a crucial role in your comfort and convenience on the road. Consider factors like the number of passengers you'll accommodate, sleeping arrangements, kitchen and bathroom facilities, and storage space. The layout should match your lifestyle and ensure everyone has enough room to move comfortably.

Establish a clear budget for your RV purchase, including the upfront cost and ongoing expenses such as fuel, maintenance, insurance, and campground fees. RVs come in a wide range of price points, from affordable pop-up campers to high-end Class A motorhomes. Be realistic about what you can afford, factoring in both the initial purchase price and the cost of ownership over time.

Consider whether you'll buy new or used, as used RVs can offer significant cost savings.

Assessing your towing capacity is crucial if you're considering a travel trailer or fifth-wheel trailer. Check the towing capacity of your existing vehicle or determine if you'll need to invest in a towing vehicle. Towing capacity varies significantly depending on your vehicle's make and model, so make sure it can safely handle the RV you plan to tow.

Consider your comfort level with driving and maneuvering an RV. Larger Class A motorhomes and fifth-wheel trailers may require more experience and confidence behind the wheel, especially on narrow or winding roads. Smaller options like camper vans and travel trailers offer more excellent maneuverability, making them suitable for those new to RV travel.

RVs come with many amenities and features, including kitchens, bathrooms, entertainment systems, and climate control. Identify the must-have amenities that enhance your travel experience. Features like a generator, solar panels, slide-outs, and satellite TV can add convenience and comfort but also affect your RV's overall weight, cost, and maintenance requirements.

Consider the maintenance and repair needs of the RV you're considering. Newer RVs may require less immediate maintenance, while older ones may have more potential issues. Evaluate your willingness and ability to handle maintenance tasks or budget for professional repairs. Keeping your RV in good condition is essential to ensure safety and longevity.

Think about the type of campgrounds and RV parks you plan to visit. Some campgrounds have size restrictions, limited hookups, or challenging terrain. Make sure your chosen RV can comfortably navigate and fit within the campgrounds you intend to visit. Smaller RVs have more flexibility in this regard, allowing you to access a broader range of camping locations.

While it may seem premature, considering the RV's resale value is wise, especially if you anticipate upgrading or changing your RV in the future. Some RV brands and models hold their value better than others, so researching the resale market can help you make a more financially sound decision.

In conclusion, selecting the right RV involves carefully assessing your travel needs, preferences, and resources. Choosing the type, size, layout, and amenities that align with your lifestyle and budget is paramount. Equally important is considering the practical aspects of maintenance, towing, maneuverability, and campground accessibility. By carefully evaluating these factors, prospective RV owners can make an informed choice that enhances their RV travel experience and ensures years of memorable adventures on the open road.

Budgeting for your RV adventure

Embarking on an RV adventure is an exciting prospect, offering the allure of freedom, exploration, and the chance to connect with nature and culture. However, effective budgeting is crucial to enjoying the journey and avoiding financial stress fully. Budgeting for your RV adventure involves meticulous planning, consideration of various expenses, and balancing comfort and cost efficiency. This section explores the key aspects of budgeting for your RV adventure, helping you prepare for a memorable and financially sustainable journey on the open road.

The first step in budgeting for your RV adventure is considering the upfront costs. This includes the purchase price of the RV itself, which can vary greatly depending on the vehicle's type, size, and age. Newer RVs tend to be more expensive, while used options can provide cost savings. Additionally, factor in any necessary accessories or equipment costs, such as towing vehicles, camping gear, or RV-specific insurance.

Fuel is a significant expense for RV travelers, especially for larger motorhomes or towing vehicles. Calculate your estimated fuel consumption based on your RV's mileage per gallon and your travel distance. Fuel prices can vary widely across regions and seasons, so it's essential to budget for fluctuations in fuel costs.

RV campgrounds offer a range of amenities, from basic sites with minimal facilities to luxury resorts with full hookups, pools, and entertainment options. Research campground fees in advance and consider your preferences. Some RVers opt for boondocking or dry camping, which involves staying in free or low-cost locations without hookups, to reduce campground expenses.

RVs, like any vehicle, require regular maintenance and occasional repairs. Budget for routine maintenance tasks such as oil changes, tire replacements, and generator servicing. Additionally, set aside funds for unexpected repairs, as breakdowns can happen anytime. Establishing an emergency fund specifically for RV repairs is a wise financial move.

Food is a variable expense that can be managed based on your dining preferences. Some RVers cook meals in their RVs to save on restaurant costs, while others enjoy the occasional dining out experience. Budget for groceries, dining out, and any camping supplies or equipment you may need, such as propane for cooking, outdoor furniture, or camping accessories.

Part of the RV adventure is exploring new destinations and enjoying recreational activities. Plan for entertainment expenses, including park entrance fees, outdoor excursions, guided tours, or cultural experiences. Research the costs of activities in the areas you plan to visit and allocate funds accordingly.

Some RVers opt to join membership programs or clubs that offer discounts on campground fees, fuel, and other travel-related expenses. While these memberships can provide cost savings over time, there are upfront fees associated with joining. Evaluate whether the benefits of membership align with your travel plans and budget.

RV insurance is necessary to protect your investment and provide liability coverage while on the road. Premiums can vary depending on factors such as the type and value of your RV, your driving history, and the coverage options you choose. Obtain insurance quotes from multiple providers to find the best coverage at a competitive rate.

Be prepared for unexpected or miscellaneous expenses that may arise during your RV adventure. This includes vehicle registration fees, tolls, laundry, and personal expenses. Creating a miscellaneous category in your budget allows you to account for unforeseen costs without derailing your financial plan.

While creating a detailed budget is essential, it's equally important to allow for flexibility. Unexpected opportunities or changes in plans may arise, and having some financial leeway can enhance your RV adventure. Consider setting aside a portion of your budget as a contingency fund to cover unforeseen circumstances or to indulge in spontaneous experiences.

Monitoring your expenses during your RV adventure is vital to staying within your budget. Use digital tools, apps, or a traditional pen-and-paper method to track your spending. Regularly review your budget to assess whether adjustments are needed, especially if unexpected expenses occur.

In conclusion, budgeting for your RV adventure is fundamental to ensuring a financially sustainable and enjoyable journey. Effective budgeting involves carefully considering upfront costs, ongoing expenses, and contingencies. It also requires balancing comfort and cost efficiency to make the most of your RV adventure. By planning and managing your finances thoughtfully, you can embark on a fulfilling and financially responsible RV adventure, allowing you to savor the freedom of the open road without financial worries.

Tips for buying or renting the right RV for your needs

The world of recreational vehicles (RVs) offers endless opportunities for adventure and exploration, whether you're planning a cross-country road trip, a weekend getaway, or a camping excursion. However, choosing the right RV for your needs can be a daunting task with numerous options available in the market. Whether you're considering buying or renting an RV, making an informed decision that aligns with your preferences, budget, and travel goals is crucial. In this section, we will discuss some valuable tips to help you select the perfect RV that caters to your specific needs and desires.

To start, one of the most critical factors when deciding between buying or renting an RV is to evaluate your long-term commitment to RVing. Buying an RV can be a significant investment, so assessing whether you plan to use it frequently or just for occasional trips is essential. If you're a dedicated RV enthusiast who envisions multiple trips each year, buying might be a sensible choice as it provides long-term cost savings compared to renting. On the other hand, if you're new to RVing or prefer the flexibility of not owning a large vehicle, renting is an excellent way to dip your toes into the RV lifestyle without a substantial upfront expense.

Next, you must consider the size and type of RV that suits your needs. RVs come in various shapes and sizes, from compact campervans to spacious motorhomes and fifth-wheel trailers. Your choice should align with the number of travelers, the amount of storage space required, and the level of comfort you desire during your journeys. Families with children may prefer larger RVs with multiple sleeping areas, while solo travelers or couples may find smaller models more practical and maneuverable. Consider your travel style and preferences when deciding on the size and type of RV that will provide the best adventure experience.

Your budget is another essential aspect to weigh when buying or renting an RV. Determine how much you're willing to invest in this mode of travel, considering not only the purchase or rental price but also ongoing expenses such as fuel, maintenance, insurance, and campground fees. When buying, consider new and used RVs, as used units can often provide excellent value and save you significant money. Renting allows you to budget for specific trips without the financial commitment of ownership, making it a more cost-effective choice for some.

Before making a decision, thoroughly research RV dealerships, rental agencies, and online marketplaces to compare prices and options. Remember that there may be seasonal variations in rental rates, so planning your trip during the off-peak season could result in more affordable rental fees. Similarly, purchasing an RV during a dealership's clearance sale or at a RV show can lead to significant savings.

Moreover, the layout and amenities inside the RV play a crucial role in determining its suitability for your needs. Think about your daily routines and the features that will make your travels comfortable and enjoyable. Consider factors such as the kitchen layout, bathroom facilities, sleeping arrangements, and entertainment options. Some RVs come equipped with luxuries like full-size kitchens, spacious showers, and entertainment systems, while others offer more basic amenities. Carefully assess your requirements and prioritize the features that matter most to you.

Another factor to consider is the RV's driving and handling characteristics. Larger motorhomes and fifth-wheel trailers may require more experience and confidence behind the wheel, while smaller campervans and travel trailers are typically easier to maneuver. If you're new to RVing, starting with a smaller and more manageable unit is advisable, especially if you plan to drive through narrow roads or navigate tight campsites. Additionally, consider the fuel efficiency of the RV, as larger models tend to consume more fuel, impacting both your budget and the environmental footprint of your travels.

Safety is paramount when selecting an RV, whether for purchase or rental. Ensure that the RV you choose complies with safety standards and has essential safety features such as working seatbelts, smoke detectors, fire extinguishers, and carbon monoxide alarms. If you're renting, thoroughly inspect the RV's condition before accepting it, and familiarize yourself with emergency procedures and the location of safety equipment. Your peace of mind and the well-being of your fellow travelers should never be compromised.

Regarding RV maintenance and repairs, it's vital to be prepared. Like any other vehicles, RVs require regular upkeep to ensure they operate safely and efficiently. Before deciding, research the maintenance requirements of the specific RV model you're considering. Consider whether you have the skills and tools to perform basic maintenance tasks yourself or if you'll rely on professional services. Some individuals find the do-it-yourself approach rewarding and cost-effective, while others prefer the convenience of leaving maintenance to experts.

Finally, don't underestimate the importance of RV insurance and campground accessibility. RV insurance can vary significantly in terms of coverage and cost, so obtain quotes from multiple providers to find the best policy for your needs. Additionally, research campgrounds and RV parks in the areas you plan to visit, as not all locations are suitable for all types and sizes of RVs. Check for availability, amenities, and any restrictions that may apply, such as maximum RV length or pet policies.

In conclusion, choosing the right RV for your needs is a significant decision that requires careful consideration of various factors. Whether you opt to buy or rent, assess your commitment to RVing, budget constraints, size requirements, and desired amenities. Safety, maintenance, and insurance should never be overlooked, and thorough research is essential to finding the best adventure options. With these tips in mind, you can confidently embark on your RV journey, knowing you've chosen the perfect RV to create unforgettable memories and experiences.

CHAPTER III

Preparing for the Journey

Planning your national park road trip

The allure of America's national parks beckons adventurers from all corners of the world. These pristine landscapes offer a chance to connect with nature, witness breathtaking scenery, and immerse oneself in the wonders of the great outdoors. Planning a national park road trip is an exhilarating endeavor that requires thoughtful preparation to ensure a memorable and enjoyable experience. This section will delve into the essential steps to consider when planning your national park road trip, from selecting destinations and mapping your route to understanding park regulations and embracing responsible tourism.

To embark on a thriving national park road trip, the first step is choosing your destinations. The United States boasts an array of national parks, each with its unique beauty and attractions. Research and prioritize the parks that align with your interests, whether you're drawn to the majestic mountains of Rocky Mountain National Park, the iconic geysers of Yellowstone, or the stunning red rock formations of Arches National Park. Consider factors such as the time of year you plan to travel, the activities you wish to partake in (hiking, camping, wildlife viewing), and the level of solitude or crowd tolerance you prefer. Your chosen destinations will form the foundation of your road trip adventure.

Once you've identified your target national parks, it's time to map out your route. National parks are often dispersed across vast regions, and the distances between them can be substantial. Use online mapping tools or GPS devices to plot your course, considering the driving time between parks, the availability of accommodations, and the scenic routes you'd like to explore along the way. Be mindful of the season and weather conditions, as some park roads may be closed during winter. A well-thought-out itinerary will help you make the most of your journey and ensure you don't miss any must-see attractions en route.

Accommodations are a crucial aspect of your road trip planning. National parks offer various lodging options, from campgrounds and RV parks to cabins and lodges. Consider your comfort preferences, budget, and the required amenities when choosing your accommodations. Camping enthusiasts may relish the opportunity to sleep under the stars in the park's campgrounds, while those seeking a bit more comfort can opt for lodge or cabin stays. Make reservations well in advance, especially during peak tourist seasons, to secure your preferred accommodations and campsite.

Understanding park regulations and rules is essential to ensure your visit is both safe and respectful of the natural environment. National parks have specific camping, hiking, wildlife interactions, and waste disposal guidelines. Familiarize yourself with these rules, and adhere to Leave No Trace principles to minimize your impact on the ecosystem. It's also advisable to check for any park alerts or advisories on the official park websites before your trip, as conditions can change, and temporary closures may be in effect due to wildfires, weather, or other factors.

Preparing for outdoor activities is another critical aspect of planning your national park road trip. National parks offer many recreational opportunities, from hiking and biking to wildlife watching and stargazing. Research the trails and activities available in each park, and assess your fitness level and interests to select suitable options. Ensure you have the necessary gear and equipment for your chosen activities, such as hiking boots, backpacks, binoculars, and wildlife identification guides. It's also wise to check the weather forecast and be prepared for varying conditions, as the weather in national parks can be unpredictable.

Safety should be a top priority throughout your road trip. Inform a trusted friend or family member of your travel itinerary and share your expected return date with them. Carry a well-stocked first aid kit, emergency supplies, and ample water and snacks in your vehicle. Cell phone reception may be unreliable in remote areas, so consider investing in a satellite phone or a personal locator beacon for added security. Familiarize yourself with the location of the nearest medical facilities and emergency contacts in each park you visit.

Responsible tourism is crucial when exploring national parks. These protected areas' natural beauty and delicate ecosystems rely on visitors to minimize their impact. Stay on designated trails, avoid disturbing wildlife, and dispose of trash properly. Respect the rules about campfires and adhere to fire bans and restrictions. Avoid disturbing fragile environments, such as cryptobiotic soil crusts found in desert parks. Your actions can make a significant difference in preserving these national treasures for future generations.

Budgeting for your national park road trip is an aspect that shouldn't be overlooked. While entrance fees to national parks are relatively affordable, additional expenses can add up. Consider costs such as gas, accommodations, food, park passes, and activity fees when setting your budget. Look for ways to save money, such as purchasing an annual America the Beautiful pass, which grants access to all national parks and federal recreation sites for a year, or opting for affordable camping and cooking your meals.

Finally, flexibility is key to a successful national park road trip. While having a well-structured itinerary is necessary, be open to unexpected detours and discoveries along the way. National parks are full of hidden gems and off-the-beaten-path attractions that may not be in your initial plan. Allow yourself the freedom to explore and embrace the spontaneity of the journey.

In conclusion, planning a national park road trip is a thrilling undertaking that requires meticulous preparation and a deep appreciation for the natural world. Select your destinations wisely, map out your route, secure accommodations, and understand park regulations to ensure a smooth and fulfilling adventure. Be prepared for outdoor activities, prioritize safety, and practice responsible tourism to impact these pristine environments positively. With careful planning and an open mind, your national park road trip promises to be a remarkable and transformative experience, connecting you with the breathtaking beauty of America's wild places.

Creating a travel itinerary

The freedom of the open road, the flexibility to explore at your own pace, and the comfort of a home on wheels are just a few reasons why RV travel is a beloved way to experience the world. Whether you're planning a cross-country adventure, a scenic route along the coast, or a journey to visit national parks, creating a travel itinerary for your RV trip is vital to ensure a memorable and stress- free experience. This section will delve into the essential elements of crafting a well-structured itinerary for your RV adventure, from setting objectives and selecting destinations to planning routes and incorporating flexibility.

To start, it's crucial to establish clear objectives for your RV trip. What are your goals and expectations? Are you seeking relaxation and leisure, or is your trip focused on exploration and adventure? Do you want to visit specific landmarks, natural wonders, or cultural attractions? You can tailor your itinerary to meet your unique desires and preferences by defining your objectives. Whether it's a leisurely journey through wine country, a quest to see all the national parks, or an off-the-beaten-path exploration, knowing your purpose will guide your planning process.

Selecting destinations is the next critical step in creating your RV travel itinerary. Consider the places you've always dreamed of visiting and the experiences you want to have. Some travelers prefer the convenience of established campgrounds with amenities, while others seek solitude in more remote locations. Research potential destinations to determine if they align with your interests and needs. National parks, state parks, scenic byways, and coastal routes offer a wealth of options for RV travelers. Make a list of your must-see destinations, and then prioritize them based on your interests and the available time.

Planning your routes and estimating driving times are essential aspects of your itinerary. RV travel often involves longer driving days compared to other modes of transportation, so it's essential to plan your routes carefully to avoid exhaustion and make the most of your journey. Utilize GPS navigation devices, online mapping tools, or specialized RV trip planning apps to map out your routes, considering the distance between destinations and the type of roads you'll be traversing. Be realistic about driving times and incorporate breaks to rest and explore along the way. Remember that RVs may have speed and length restrictions on certain roads, so plan accordingly.

Accommodations play a significant role in your RV travel experience. Decide whether you'll stay in campgrounds, RV parks, or other accommodations. Research and make early reservations, especially during peak travel seasons when campgrounds may fill up quickly. Consider factors such as the availability of hookups (water, electricity, sewage), campground amenities (showers, restrooms, laundry facilities), and proximity to your chosen destinations. Budget for camping fees in your itinerary can vary widely depending on the location and the level of amenities provided.

Incorporate flexibility into your itinerary to make the most of your RV trip. While planning is essential, leaving room for spontaneity can lead to unexpected discoveries and memorable experiences. Allow for unscheduled stops, detours, and last-minute changes to your plans. Some of the most cherished moments of RV travel often come from impromptu interactions with locals, scenic overlooks, or hidden gems you stumble upon during your journey. Flexibility ensures that your trip remains enjoyable and stress-free.

Safety and preparedness should be top priorities when creating your RV travel itinerary. Before hitting the road, ensure your RV is in good working condition by performing necessary maintenance and safety checks. Familiarize yourself with the RV's systems and how to operate them. Carry essential safety equipment, including a fire extinguisher, first aid kit, emergency tools, and a roadside assistance plan. Make sure your RV is properly stocked with food, water, and supplies for your journey. Plan for contingencies, such as unexpected weather events or mechanical issues, and have a communication plan in place in case of emergencies.

Budgeting is another crucial aspect of your RV travel itinerary. Calculate the costs of fuel, campground fees, food, activities, and any other expenses you anticipate during your trip. Be mindful of your budget and look for ways to save money, such as cooking your meals in the RV or taking advantage of discount programs for campgrounds and attractions. It's essential to have a financial plan to ensure your trip remains within your means and that you can fully enjoy the experiences you've planned.

Finally, document your RV journey through photos, journals, or a travel blog. Capturing memories and reflecting on your adventures can enhance your overall travel experience and provide lasting mementos. Share your experiences with family and friends, and consider joining online RV communities and forums to connect with fellow travelers, exchange tips, and seek advice for future trips.

In conclusion, creating a travel itinerary for your RV trip is vital in ensuring a successful and enjoyable adventure. Start by setting clear objectives, selecting destinations, and planning your routes and accommodations. Incorporate flexibility into your plans, prioritize safety and preparedness, and establish a budget to manage expenses effectively. By carefully crafting your itinerary, you can embark on an RV journey that fulfills your travel dreams, creates lasting memories, and allows you to embrace the freedom of the open road.

Packing essentials for RV travel

Embarking on an RV adventure is a thrilling and liberating experience, offering the chance to explore the great outdoors while enjoying the comforts of home on wheels. Packaging the right essentials is crucial to make the most of your journey and ensure a smooth and enjoyable RV trip. Whether you're a seasoned RV traveler or planning your first excursion, this section will guide you through the essential items to include in your packing list, from practical tools and safety equipment to personal items and camping gear.

First and foremost, safety should be a top priority when packing for your RV trip. Start by ensuring you have all the necessary documents, including your driver's license, vehicle registration, insurance information, and any required permits for the places you plan to visit. It's also a good practice to carry a printed copy of your itinerary with contact information for emergency contacts. In terms of safety equipment, a well-stocked first aid kit should be a non-negotiable item in your RV. Include bandages, antiseptic wipes, pain relievers, adhesive tape, scissors, tweezers, and any prescription medications you may need.

Fire safety is of utmost importance in an RV. Ensure your RV is equipped with working smoke detectors and a fire extinguisher, and familiarize yourself with their locations and usage. Pack a compact and easy-to-store collapsible ladder that can be used to escape through windows in case of emergencies. Additionally, have a clear exit plan for all passengers on board.

To keep your RV running smoothly during your journey, consider packing a basic toolkit with essential tools such as screwdrivers, pliers, wrenches, and a tire pressure gauge. Familiarize yourself with your RV's systems and how to perform basic maintenance tasks, like checking fluid levels and changing fuses. Having the right tools can save you time and money on the road.

When it comes to personal items, remember to pack all necessary toiletries, including soap, shampoo, toothpaste, and toilet paper. Don't forget prescription eyewear, contact lenses, or any other medical supplies you require. Pack appropriate clothing for various weather conditions depending on your destination and the activities you plan to undertake. Layering is key for versatility, and moisture-wicking and quick-drying fabrics are ideal for outdoor activities. Don't forget comfortable shoes suitable for walking and hiking.

In the kitchen area of your RV, ensure you have all the essential cooking and dining supplies. A set of pots, pans, utensils, dishes, and cookware is essential. Depending on your cooking style, you may also want to bring a portable grill or camp stove for outdoor cooking. Pack basic pantry staples like cooking oil, spices, condiments, and non-perishable food items to have on hand for quick and easy meals.

Cleanliness and sanitation are vital during your RV journey. Stock up on cleaning supplies, including dish soap, sponges, and trash bags. Consider bringing a portable waste disposal system, especially if you plan to camp in locations without hookups. A collapsible water container and a water filtration system can be useful for freshwater supply, especially when boondocking or camping in remote areas.

Don't forget bedding essentials to ensure a comfortable and restful night's sleep. Pack sheets, blankets, and pillows to suit your preferences and the sleeping arrangements in your RV. Consider a comfortable mattress topper for added comfort if your RV has a separate bedroom area. Additionally, earplugs and sleep masks can be useful for light sleepers or when camping in noisy locations.

Entertainment and leisure items can enhance your RV experience during downtime. Bring along books, board games, playing cards, or any other hobbies you enjoy. Consider a portable music player or a Bluetooth speaker for music and podcasts. Depending on your interests, outdoor gear such as bicycles, kayaks, or fishing equipment can add to your recreational options.

It's essential to have the right gear for outdoor activities and exploring. Bring appropriate hiking boots, backpacks, and poles if you plan to hike. For water activities, pack life jackets, swimwear, and snorkeling gear if you intend to explore aquatic environments. Don't forget sunscreen, insect repellent, and a good quality backpack to carry essentials during your outdoor adventures.

When packing your RV, organization is key. Use storage containers, shelves, and hooks to maximize space and keep items tidy and accessible. Secure loose items to prevent them from shifting during travel and potentially causing damage or creating hazards. Consider investing in collapsible or space-saving items to optimize your RV's limited storage space.

Finally, take some time to review your packing list and ensure you've covered all the essentials specific to your trip. Different RV trips may require additional items, such as winter gear for cold-weather travel or beach gear for coastal adventures. Customize your packing list to align with your destination, season, and activities planned.

In conclusion, packing for an RV trip requires careful consideration of safety, comfort, and practicality. Be prepared with essential safety equipment, tools, and documentation. Prioritize personal items and clothing, as well as kitchen and camping gear. With proper organization and thoughtful packing, you can embark on your RV adventure well-prepared and ready to enjoy the freedom of the open road.

Safety and maintenance checks before hitting the road

Before embarking on any road trip, especially one in an RV, it is crucial to prioritize safety and perform thorough maintenance checks on your vehicle. RV travel offers the freedom to explore diverse landscapes and enjoy the comforts of home on wheels, but ensuring the safety of both you and your passengers is paramount. This section will explore the essential safety and maintenance checks that should be conducted before hitting the road in your RV, from inspecting the vehicle's mechanical systems to verifying safety equipment and preparing for emergencies.

First and foremost, safety should be a top priority when preparing for your RV trip. Start by thoroughly inspecting the mechanical systems of your RV. Check the engine, transmission, brakes, tires, and suspension. Ensure that all fluids (engine oil, transmission fluid, brake fluid, coolant, and power steering fluid) are at the appropriate levels and free of leaks. Replace worn-out or damaged components, such as brake pads or tires, as needed. Regularly service your RV's engine and transmission according to the manufacturer's recommendations. A well-maintained engine improves fuel efficiency and reduces the risk of breakdowns on the road.

The condition of your RV's tires is critical to both safety and fuel efficiency. Inspect the tires for signs of wear, including uneven tread or sidewall damage. Ensure that they are properly inflated according to the manufacturer's specifications. Overinflated or underinflated tires can affect handling and fuel economy. Don't forget to check the spare tire and ensure you have the necessary tools to change a flat tire if needed.

RVs are heavier and require longer stopping distances than typical passenger vehicles. Have your brakes inspected and serviced regularly to ensure they are in optimal condition. If you notice any signs of brake problems, such as squeaking, grinding, or reduced braking performance, address them promptly. Well-maintained brakes are essential for your safety and that of other road users.

A well-functioning suspension and steering system are crucial for stability and control while driving your RV. Inspect the shocks, struts, and steering components for signs of wear or damage. Address any issues promptly to maintain safe handling and prevent accidents.

Ensure that all the lights on your RV are in working order, including headlights, taillights, brake lights, turn signals, and hazard lights. Non-functioning lights can lead to accidents or traffic violations. Test your RV's electrical systems, including batteries, generator, and power outlets, to ensure they function correctly and provide the necessary power for appliances and lighting during your trip.

Many RVs use propane for cooking, heating, and refrigeration. Check all propane lines, connections, and appliances for leaks or damage. Verify that propane detectors and alarms are in working order. A propane leak can pose a significant safety risk, so addressing any issues promptly is crucial.

Ensure your RV is equipped with essential safety equipment, including smoke detectors, carbon monoxide detectors, and fire extinguishers. Test these devices to ensure they are functional and replace batteries or devices that have reached their expiration dates. Familiarize yourself with their locations and operation. Additionally, consider investing in a quality fire escape ladder for emergency exits.

Before hitting the road, make sure you have reliable communication tools and navigation systems. A working cell phone with a charged battery is essential for emergencies and staying connected. Consider a GPS device or navigation app to help you plan routes and avoid getting lost. It's also a good idea to carry physical maps as a backup in case of technology failures.

Depending on the season and your destination, your RV may encounter various weather conditions. Ensure your vehicle is prepared for the elements by checking windshield wipers, defrosters, and heating and cooling systems. Have winter-ready equipment such as tire chains and snow brushes if you plan to travel in colder regions.

Assemble a comprehensive emergency kit that includes items like flashlights, batteries, a multi-tool, a first aid kit, non-perishable food, water, blankets, and essential medications. Keep this kit easily accessible inside your RV. In the event of a breakdown or unexpected situation, having these supplies on hand can be a lifesaver.

Before you hit the road, share your travel itinerary and contact information with a trusted friend or family member. Provide details about your planned route, destinations, and expected return date. This information can be invaluable in case of emergencies or if you need assistance during your trip.

In conclusion, conducting thorough safety and maintenance checks before hitting the road in your RV is essential for a smooth and secure journey. Regular maintenance, attention to safety equipment, and emergency preparedness will help ensure your RV travel experience is enjoyable and trouble-free. By prioritizing safety, you can explore the wonders of the open road with confidence and peace of mind.

CHAPTER IV

Hitting the Road

Tips for navigating RV-friendly routes

Recreational vehicles, or RVs, offer a unique and adventurous way to explore the world. Whether you're a seasoned RVer or just embarking on your first journey, one of the most crucial aspects of your trip is planning and navigating the right routes. An RV's dimensions and specific requirements make it essential to choose RV-friendly routes to ensure a safe and enjoyable journey. This section will explore some valuable tips to help you navigate RV-friendly routes successfully.

First and foremost, it's essential to plan your route in advance. The adage "failing to plan is planning to fail" holds true for RV travel. Use technology, such as GPS devices or RV-specific navigation apps, to map your journey. These tools can help you identify routes that accommodate your RV's size and weight restrictions, avoiding roads with low clearances, narrow passages, or weight limits that your RV may exceed.

Another crucial tip is to stay informed about road conditions and closures. RV travel often takes you through diverse landscapes and weather conditions. To ensure a smooth journey, check for road closures, construction zones, or weather-related hazards before you hit the road. Websites, apps, or even local authorities can provide updates on road conditions, allowing you to adjust your route accordingly and avoid any unexpected delays or detours.

Consider the time of year when planning your RV adventure. Seasonal variations can greatly impact road conditions and accessibility. Winter weather, for example, can create icy and treacherous roads, making it essential to equip your RV with snow chains and choose regularly plowed and maintained routes. Alternatively, traveling during the summer may expose you to high temperatures and wildfire risks, necessitating route adjustments to avoid areas prone to wildfires.

While planning your RV-friendly route, consider your personal preferences and interests. If you're an outdoor enthusiast, you might want to explore national parks and scenic byways. In this case, it's essential to research RV campgrounds and campsites along your chosen route, as not all parks and scenic areas can accommodate RVs. Additionally, some parks have size restrictions, so knowing your RV's dimensions is crucial to avoid disappointment upon arrival.

When navigating RV-friendly routes, consider your RV's size and weight. RVs come in various shapes and sizes, from compact camper vans to large motorhomes. The larger your RV, the more cautious you should be when choosing routes. Pay close attention to bridge heights, as low clearances can pose a significant risk to taller RVs. Investing in a height measuring device or relying on dedicated RV navigation systems that provide information on bridge heights and weight restrictions is advisable.

Incorporate rest stops and breaks into your route planning. Long stretches of driving can be exhausting, and it's essential to rest and refuel not only for your own safety but also for the well-being of your RV. RVs require more frequent maintenance and fuel stops than regular vehicles. Ensure you plan for rest areas and gas stations that can accommodate your RV's size, and consider taking breaks to explore local attractions and enjoy the journey rather than focusing solely on the destination.

Safety should always be a top priority when navigating RV-friendly routes. Always obey speed limits, drive at a safe and comfortable pace, and avoid aggressive maneuvers. Keep a safe following distance, as RVs have longer stopping distances than regular vehicles. If you're new to RV driving, consider taking a defensive driving course specific to RVs to enhance your skills and confidence on the road.

In addition to safe driving practices, it's essential to be prepared for emergencies. Carry essential tools, spare parts, and a first-aid kit in your RV. Familiarize yourself with your RV's systems and how to perform basic maintenance tasks. In case of unexpected breakdowns or accidents, investing in roadside assistance coverage can also provide peace of mind.

Lastly, remember to enjoy the journey. RV travel offers a unique opportunity to explore diverse landscapes, meet new people, and create lasting memories. Embrace the spontaneity of the road and be open to new experiences. Engage with fellow RVers and take advantage of the RV community, which often shares valuable insights and tips for navigating RV-friendly routes.

In conclusion, navigating RV-friendly routes is crucial to a successful RV adventure. Planning your route in advance, staying informed about road conditions, considering the time of year, and considering your RV's size and weight are essential steps to ensure a safe and enjoyable journey. Rest stops, prioritizing safety, and being prepared for emergencies are key elements of a smooth RV travel experience. Ultimately, the journey itself is as important as the destination, so make the most of your RV adventure and savor the moments along the way.

The RV lifestyle: What to expect on the road

The RV lifestyle, with its promise of freedom and adventure, has been captivating the imaginations of travelers for decades. Whether you are considering hitting the road full-time or planning an extended road trip, embarking on the RV lifestyle is a thrilling and transformative journey. This section will explore what you can expect when living or traveling in an RV, from the joys of exploring new places to the challenges of life on the road.

One of the most enticing aspects of the RV lifestyle is the sense of wanderlust it satisfies. RVers can choose their destinations, change their plans at a moment's notice, and wake up to breathtaking natural landscapes or vibrant cityscapes. The possibilities are endless, and the road becomes your canvas for adventure. Whether you prefer camping in national parks, parking by serene lakes, or exploring bustling urban centers, the RV lifestyle offers a variety of experiences to satisfy all tastes.

Living in an RV also fosters a strong connection with nature. RVers often find themselves surrounded by stunning natural beauty, with the opportunity to hike in pristine wilderness, enjoy campfires under starry skies, and wake up to the sound of birdsong. The RV lifestyle encourages a deeper appreciation for the environment and a desire to live in harmony with nature. Many RVers become avid outdoor enthusiasts, taking up activities like hiking, kayaking, and birdwatching as they explore the great outdoors.

While the RV lifestyle can be enriching, it's also essential to be prepared for its challenges. Limited space is one of the most significant adjustments for those transitioning to RV living. RVs come in various sizes, but all have constrained living quarters compared to traditional homes. Effective organization and downsizing become critical skills as you must maximize your available space. Learning to live with less and prioritize what truly matters becomes a valuable lesson in the RV lifestyle.

Maintenance and upkeep of the RV is another essential aspect of life on the road. RVs are mechanical and electrical systems on wheels, and they require regular maintenance to ensure safe and trouble-free travel. Understanding your RV's systems and learning basic maintenance tasks is essential. Breakdowns and repairs are part of the RV journey, so having some mechanical knowledge or being willing to learn can save you both time and money.

Moreover, the RV lifestyle necessitates careful financial planning. While it can be more cost-effective than traditional living in some cases, it's crucial to budget for fuel, campsite fees, maintenance, insurance, and other expenses associated with RV living. Some RVers choose to work remotely or take on seasonal jobs to sustain their lifestyle on the road. A frugal approach and financial discipline are key to maintaining a comfortable and stress-free RV lifestyle.

Another aspect of the RV lifestyle to consider is the social aspect. RVers often form a tight-knit community on the road. Campgrounds and RV parks are excellent places to meet like-minded individuals and share stories, tips, and experiences. Many RVers participate in organized events and gatherings, further enhancing their sense of community. However, the transient nature of the lifestyle can also lead to frequent goodbyes, as fellow RVers move on to new destinations. It's essential to balance the desire for solitude and social interaction according to your preferences.

Healthcare and medical considerations are another vital aspect of the RV lifestyle. Access to medical facilities can vary significantly depending on your location, and emergencies can be challenging to navigate in remote areas. RVers often need to plan ahead for their healthcare needs, including maintaining health insurance, locating healthcare providers along their route, and carrying essential medications and first-aid supplies.

The RV lifestyle also involves a degree of adaptability. Plans can change due to unforeseen circumstances, weather conditions, or personal preferences. Flexibility is a valuable trait in an RVer, as it allows you to make the most of your journey and find hidden gems along the way. Embracing spontaneity and going with the flow can lead to some of the most memorable experiences on the road.

In conclusion, the RV lifestyle offers a unique blend of freedom, adventure, and challenges. It provides the opportunity to explore the world, connect with nature, and build a sense of community with fellow travelers. However, it also requires careful planning, organization, financial discipline, and adaptability. The RV lifestyle is not for everyone, but for those who choose to embark on this journey, it can be a life-changing and enriching experience. Whether you're seeking adventure, a change of pace, or a deeper connection with the natural world, the RV lifestyle offers a less traveled road waiting to be explored.

Managing your travel budget

Embarking on an RV trip is an exciting adventure that offers the freedom to explore new places and create lasting memories. However, managing your travel budget is critical to ensuring a successful and enjoyable journey. Whether you are a full-time RVer or planning a short road trip, wise financial planning can make all the difference. In this section, we will explore essential tips and strategies for effectively managing your travel budget on your RV trip.

Setting a realistic budget is one of the first steps in budget management for an RV trip. Determine how much you are willing to spend on various aspects of your journey, such as fuel, campsite fees, food, entertainment, and maintenance. Be sure to account for unexpected expenses as well. Setting a budget provides a clear financial framework and helps you make informed decisions throughout your trip.

Fuel expenses are a significant portion of an RV travel budget. Consider investing in a fuel-efficient RV or adopting fuel-saving driving habits to save on fuel costs. Maintaining a steady speed, avoiding excessive idling, and properly inflating your RV's tires can improve fuel efficiency. Additionally, plan your routes wisely to minimize unnecessary driving and fuel consumption.

Campsite fees can vary widely depending on the type of campgrounds you choose. Full-service RV parks tend to be more expensive, while boondocking or dry camping in free or low-cost locations can help you save money. Research campgrounds in advance, and consider a mix of options to balance convenience and cost. Many RVers also invest in memberships or discount programs like Passport America or Good Sam to access reduced campsite fees.

Food expenses can add up quickly during an RV trip, especially if you dine out frequently. Plan your meals in advance and prepare your own food whenever possible to stay within budget. RVs are equipped with kitchens, making cooking and storing meals on the road easy. Stock up on groceries and essentials at local stores or farmers' markets, which can be more affordable than convenience stores or tourist areas.

Entertainment and activities are essential to any RV trip, but they can also impact your budget. Look for free or low-cost attractions in the areas you plan to visit, such as hiking trails, scenic drives, and cultural events. Take advantage of national parks and public lands, which often offer affordable admission fees and stunning natural beauty. Participating in outdoor activities like hiking, fishing, or birdwatching can also be both enjoyable and budget-friendly.

Maintenance and repairs are inevitable expenses when traveling in an RV. Regular maintenance can prevent costly breakdowns, so budgeting for routine checks and services is essential. Additionally, set aside an emergency fund for unexpected repairs. If you are handy with tools, consider learning basic RV maintenance and repair tasks to save money on labor costs.

Financial discipline is crucial while managing your travel budget on an RV trip. Avoid unnecessary expenses and impulse purchases by tracking your spending regularly. Utilize budgeting apps or spreadsheets to monitor your expenditures and compare them to your initial budget. This will help you identify areas where you may be overspending and make necessary adjustments.

Another cost-saving strategy is to take advantage of loyalty programs and discounts. Many businesses offer discounts to RVers, so inquire about discounts on fuel, groceries, and camping fees. Joining RV clubs and memberships, such as Good Sam or Escapees, can provide access to exclusive discounts and resources that can help you save money.

Healthcare considerations are also essential when managing your budget on an RV trip. Ensure you have adequate health insurance coverage, as medical emergencies can be costly. Carry essential medications and a well-stocked first-aid kit to address minor health issues on the road. Research healthcare providers and facilities along your route, so you are prepared in case of medical needs.

Flexibility and adaptability are valuable qualities for managing your travel budget. Unexpected situations may arise, such as weather-related delays or changes in plans. Having some financial flexibility in your budget can help you navigate these challenges without feeling financially stressed.

In conclusion, managing your travel budget on an RV trip requires careful planning, discipline, and resourcefulness. Setting a realistic budget, minimizing fuel expenses, choosing cost-effective campsites, preparing your own meals, and seeking out affordable entertainment are all key strategies to keep your spending in check. Additionally, budgeting for maintenance, tracking expenses, and taking advantage of discounts can further contribute to a successful and budget-friendly RV journey. By adhering to these tips and maintaining financial discipline, you can enjoy the freedom and adventure of the RV lifestyle without breaking the bank.

Finding RV-friendly campsites and accommodations

The joy of RV travel lies in the freedom it offers to explore new places and create unforgettable experiences. A crucial aspect of this adventure is finding suitable campsites and accommodations that cater to your recreational vehicle (RV) needs. Whether you're a seasoned RVer or just beginning your journey, knowing how to locate RV-friendly campsites and accommodations is essential for a smooth and enjoyable trip. This section will explore various strategies and resources to help you find the perfect places to park your RV and call it home while on the road.

One of the most reliable sources for locating RV-friendly campsites is the internet. Numerous websites and apps are dedicated to helping RVers find suitable accommodations. Websites like RV Park Reviews, Campendium, and AllStays provide comprehensive information on RV campgrounds and parks across the country. These platforms offer user-generated reviews, ratings, and essential details such as site amenities, fees, and contact information, making it easier to make informed decisions when choosing a place to stay.

Another valuable online resource is the National Park Service (NPS) official website. National parks offer some of the country's most breathtaking natural settings, and many have RV-friendly campgrounds. The NPS website provides information about each park's RV facilities, including site availability, size restrictions, and reservation options. Planning your RV trip around national parks can lead to unforgettable experiences in the heart of nature.

State parks are also excellent options for RV-friendly accommodations. Each state typically has its own website with detailed information about state park campgrounds and their suitability for RVs. State parks often offer a mix of camping experiences, from full-hookup sites with amenities to more rustic and primitive campgrounds. Researching state park options in the regions you plan to visit can help you find affordable and scenic RV accommodations.

Private RV campgrounds and resorts are widely available throughout the United States for those seeking more convenience and amenities. These establishments cater specifically to RV travelers and offer various services, including full hookups, laundry facilities, recreational activities, and on-site convenience stores. Websites like KOA (Kampgrounds of America) and Good Sam Club provide directories of private campgrounds and RV parks, complete with detailed information and member reviews.

Another popular option for RVers is boondocking or dry camping. Boondocking refers to camping in undeveloped areas without hookups, often on public lands managed by agencies like the Bureau of Land Management (BLM) or the U.S. Forest Service. While boondocking offers a more rustic experience, it can be gratifying, providing opportunities for solitude and immersion in nature. Apps like Campendium and FreeCampsites.net list free and low-cost boondocking locations, making it easier to find suitable spots.

When planning your RV journey, consider the specific needs of your RV. RVs come in various sizes and configurations, and not all campsites can accommodate larger rigs or offer the required amenities. Pay attention to size restrictions, hookups (water, electricity, sewage), and accessibility when selecting your accommodations. Contact campgrounds or RV parks in advance to inquire about availability and any specific requirements.

Flexibility in your travel plans can also enhance your ability to find RV-friendly accommodations. While it's advisable to make reservations for popular destinations or during peak travel seasons, having the flexibility to adjust your itinerary can open up opportunities to discover hidden gems. Last-minute availability at campgrounds or private RV parks may offer unique and unexpected experiences along your route.

Networking within the RV community is another valuable strategy for finding great accommodations. Online forums, social media groups, and RVing clubs provide platforms for RVers to share recommendations and insights about their favorite places to stay. Engaging with fellow RV enthusiasts can lead to insider tips and personal recommendations you won't find in standard online directories.

Additionally, consider investing in memberships or discount programs that offer benefits to RV travelers. Programs like Passport America, Escapees, and Good Sam Club provide access to exclusive discounts and resources. These memberships can significantly save campsite fees, making your RV journey more budget-friendly.

In conclusion, finding RV-friendly campsites and accommodations is fundamental to a successful and enjoyable RV adventure. Leveraging online resources, such as dedicated websites, national park and state park websites, and directories of private campgrounds, can help you locate suitable places to park your RV. Boondocking is another option for those seeking a more rustic experience, and networking within the RV community can provide valuable recommendations and insights. With careful planning and flexibility, you can discover a wide range of RV-friendly accommodations to enhance your journey and make your RV trip a memorable experience.

CHAPTER V

Exploring National Parks

Highlights from some of the most popular national parks

The United States boasts many national parks, each offering unique natural beauty, diverse ecosystems, and recreational opportunities. From the rugged mountains of the Rockies to the serene coastlines of the Pacific, these protected areas preserve some of the country's most breathtaking landscapes and provide opportunities for outdoor enthusiasts and nature lovers alike. In this section, we will explore highlights from some of the most popular national parks, showcasing the incredible diversity and natural wonders they have to offer.

Yellowstone National Park, located primarily in Wyoming but also extending into Montana and Idaho, is renowned for its geothermal features, including the iconic Old Faithful geyser. The park's geysers, hot springs, and mudpots create a unique and otherworldly landscape. Visitors can witness the power of the Earth's geothermal activity while exploring the park's extensive network of hiking trails, waterfalls, and wildlife. Yellowstone is also home to many animals, including bison, grizzly bears, wolves, and elk, making it a premier destination for wildlife enthusiasts.

Yosemite National Park, situated in California's Sierra Nevada mountains, is celebrated for its majestic granite cliffs, pristine waterfalls, and ancient giant sequoias. The iconic El Capitan and Half Dome rock formations are popular attractions for rock climbers and hikers. Yosemite Valley, with its dramatic scenery and meandering Merced River, offers a range of outdoor activities, from hiking and camping to photography and birdwatching. Visitors can also explore the Mariposa Grove of Giant Sequoias, home to some of the largest and oldest trees on the planet.

Grand Canyon National Park in Arizona is a geological wonder that has captivated visitors for centuries. Carved by the Colorado River, the Grand Canyon exposes nearly two billion years of Earth's geological history in its layered rock formations. The park offers hiking opportunities for all skill levels, including the famous Rim-to-Rim hike that takes adventurous trekkers from one side of the canyon to the other. The Grand Canyon's expansive vistas and ever-changing colors, particularly during sunrise and sunset, create a breathtaking spectacle that is truly unforgettable.

Zion National Park in Utah is renowned for its striking red rock formations, towering cliffs, and deep canyons carved by the Virgin River. The park's centerpiece, Zion Canyon, is a popular destination for hikers and photographers. Hiking trails like Angels Landing and The Narrows offer varying degrees of challenge, leading to stunning viewpoints and pristine slot canyons. The park's shuttle system makes it easy for visitors to access some of its most iconic spots without the hassle of parking.

Great Smoky Mountains National Park, straddling the border between North Carolina and Tennessee, is known for its lush forests, misty mountain peaks, and vibrant fall foliage. It's the most visited national park in the United States, thanks to its accessibility and diverse range of activities. Visitors can explore over 800 miles of hiking trails, including the Appalachian Trail, and enjoy scenic drives along Newfound Gap Road. The park is also famous for its rich biodiversity, with countless species of plants and animals, making it a paradise for wildlife enthusiasts.

Acadia National Park in Maine combines the beauty of rugged coastline with granite peaks and serene lakes. Cadillac Mountain, the tallest peak on the East Coast, offers breathtaking sunrise views over the Atlantic Ocean. The park's carriage roads provide an extensive network of paths for hikers, cyclists, and horseback riders. Acadia's coastline features dramatic cliffs, tide pools, and sandy beaches, making it a popular destination for those seeking outdoor adventures along the ocean.

Arches National Park in Utah is a surreal desert landscape adorned with more than 2,000 natural stone arches, along with towering pinnacles and balancing rocks. The park's unique rock formations and fiery red hues create a photographer's dream. Hiking and photography are the main draws here, with trails like Delicate Arch and Landscape Arch offering spectacular vistas. The park's clear night skies also make it an excellent spot for stargazing and astrophotography.

Rocky Mountain National Park in Colorado is a haven for mountain enthusiasts. It features towering peaks, alpine lakes, and diverse ecosystems. Trail Ridge Road, the highest continuously paved road in the United States, offers breathtaking views and access to the park's high-country terrain. Hikers can explore miles of trails, while wildlife enthusiasts may spot elk, bighorn sheep, and marmots. The park's scenery is especially stunning in the fall when the aspen trees turn vibrant shades of gold.

These are just a few of the most popular national parks in the United States, each offering a unique and unforgettable experience. Whether you're interested in geothermal wonders, towering cliffs, pristine wilderness, or captivating wildlife, America's national parks have something to offer every nature lover and adventurer. Exploring these natural wonders provides an opportunity to connect with the great outdoors and gain a deeper appreciation for the beauty and diversity of the American landscape.

Lesser-known gems worth exploring

When embarking on an RV trip, it's easy to get caught up in the allure of famous tourist destinations and well-traveled routes. However, some of the most memorable experiences can be found off the beaten path, in lesser-known gems that offer unique and authentic adventures. These hidden treasures may not make it to the glossy travel brochures, but they promise to reward the intrepid traveler with beauty, serenity, and a sense of discovery that more popular destinations often cannot. In this section, we will delve into some lesser-known gems across the United States worth exploring on your next RV adventure.

One such hidden gem is the Great Sand Dunes National Park and Preserve in southern Colorado. Nestled against the rugged Sangre de Cristo Mountains, this park boasts the tallest sand dunes in North America. The surreal landscape is a playground for outdoor enthusiasts, offering sandboarding, hiking, and stargazing opportunities. Camping within the park is an excellent way to fully immerse yourself in this unique environment, where the contrast between the towering dunes and the surrounding mountains creates an awe-inspiring backdrop for your RV adventure.

For those seeking a different kind of natural wonder, the Okefenokee National Wildlife Refuge in Georgia beckons with its enchanting blackwater swamps and pristine wilderness. This lesser-known gem is a paradise for birdwatchers and wildlife enthusiasts, with alligators, turtles, and various bird species calling it home. Paddle through the quiet waterways in a kayak or canoe, or take a leisurely stroll along the boardwalk trails to get up close to the captivating beauty of this untouched ecosystem.

In the heart of the Midwest, the Badlands National Park in South Dakota stands as an underrated treasure. This rugged landscape is a geological wonder, featuring striking buttes, canyons, and spires. RV travelers can explore the park's extensive network of hiking trails and scenic drives, marveling at the colorful layers of sedimentary rock that tell a story millions of years in the making. The Badlands' isolation and stark beauty offer a profound sense of solitude and wonder, making it an ideal destination for those seeking both adventure and tranquility.

Venturing further west, the Oregon Coast offers a lesser-known coastal escape that rivals its more famous counterparts. Unlike the crowded beaches of California, the Oregon Coast boasts rugged cliffs, hidden coves, and charming seaside towns. RV parks and campgrounds are scattered along the coast, allowing travelers to wake up to the soothing sound of crashing waves. Explore the picturesque Cape Perpetua Scenic Area, hike through dense coastal forests, and marvel at the stunning sea stacks and tidal pools that dot the shoreline.

While national parks and natural wonders often steal the spotlight, historical and cultural gems can be equally rewarding to explore on an RV journey. The Acoma Pueblo in New Mexico, also known as "Sky City," is one such hidden gem. Perched atop a 367-foot sandstone mesa, this ancient Native American settlement offers a glimpse into the rich history and traditions of the Acoma people. Visitors can take guided tours of the pueblo, visit the historic mission church, and purchase exquisite pottery made by local artisans. The spiritual connection and resilience of the Acoma people make this lesser-known destination a profound cultural experience.

Heading south to Texas, the Big Bend Ranch State Park is a vast and untamed wilderness that often goes unnoticed amidst the state's more famous national parks. With its rugged terrain, towering canyons, and the meandering Rio Grande River, this park is a haven for hikers, mountain bikers, and stargazers. Camping in this remote wilderness offers unparalleled solitude and an opportunity to connect with nature in its purest form. The night skies here are some of the darkest in the country, making it an ideal location for stargazing and astrophotography.

In the northeastern United States, the Adirondack Park in New York is a hidden gem for outdoor enthusiasts. Encompassing over six million acres of pristine wilderness, the Adirondacks offer endless hiking, paddling, and camping opportunities. The park's extensive network of trails leads to hidden lakes, waterfalls, and panoramic viewpoints. RV travelers can find a variety of campgrounds nestled in the heart of this natural wonderland, providing a comfortable base from which to explore the rugged beauty of the Adirondack Mountains.

In conclusion, while the allure of famous tourist destinations is undeniable, the lesser-known gems often hold the key to truly unique and authentic RV adventures. From the towering sand dunes of Colorado to the blackwater swamps of Georgia, the rugged Badlands of South Dakota to the serene Oregon Coast, and the cultural richness of Acoma Pueblo to the untamed wilderness of Big Bend Ranch, the United States is teeming with hidden treasures waiting to be discovered. So, the next time you plan an RV trip, consider venturing off the beaten path to uncover these lesser-known gems that promise adventure, serenity, and unforgettable memories.

Activities and attractions within the parks

National and state parks hold a special place in the hearts of outdoor enthusiasts and nature lovers. These protected areas showcase the stunning beauty of our natural world and provide various activities and attractions that cater to a diverse range of interests. From hiking through lush forests and camping under starlit skies to exploring historical sites and observing wildlife in their natural habitat, the parks offer a wealth of experiences that leave visitors in awe of the wonders of nature. In this section, we will explore the various activities and attractions in these parks, emphasizing the diverse opportunities they provide for visitors to connect with the great outdoors.

Hiking is one of the quintessential activities within parks, allowing visitors to immerse themselves in the park's natural beauty while traversing a network of trails catering to all skill levels. Whether it's a leisurely stroll along a paved path or a challenging ascent up a mountain peak, hiking offers a unique perspective on the park's landscape. For instance, Acadia National Park in Maine boasts over 120 miles of hiking trails that wind through lush forests, along rugged coastlines, and up to granite summits with breathtaking panoramic views. In contrast, the Grand Canyon National Park in Arizona presents the iconic Rim-to-Rim hike, a challenging but rewarding adventure that takes you from one side of the canyon to the other, offering a profound sense of accomplishment and an opportunity to witness the geological marvel of the canyon up close.

For those seeking a more immersive experience, camping within the parks is a timeless activity allowing visitors to connect with nature. From tent camping to RV camping, there are options for all preferences and levels of comfort. Yosemite National Park in California, with its numerous campgrounds nestled in the heart of the Sierra Nevada Mountains, provides a magical setting for a night under the stars. The sound of a crackling campfire, the scent of pine trees, and the clear night skies combine to create an unforgettable camping experience that rekindles our connection to the natural world.

In addition to hiking and camping, parks often offer a rich tapestry of historical and cultural attractions. Many parks are home to ancient ruins, historic homesteads, and preserved battlefields that provide insight into the nation's heritage. For instance, Gettysburg National Military Park in Pennsylvania preserves the site of the pivotal Battle of Gettysburg during the American Civil War. Visitors can explore the battlefield, view historic artifacts, and gain a deeper understanding of this significant event in American history.

Furthermore, parks are natural sanctuaries for wildlife, making them prime locations for wildlife observation and photography. The Everglades National Park in Florida is a prime example, home to a vast array of bird species, alligators, and other unique wildlife. Guided tours and observation points within the park offer visitors the chance to witness these creatures in their natural habitat, providing a deeper appreciation for the ecosystem's delicate balance.

Stargazing is another activity that flourishes within the tranquility of our national and state parks. With minimal light pollution and expansive night skies, these protected areas are ideal settings for astronomical observation. Bryce Canyon National Park in Utah is renowned for its dark skies and annual astronomy festivals, allowing visitors to peer into the cosmos and witness the brilliance of the Milky Way stretching across the horizon. The sense of wonder and awe inspired by stargazing in such locations is unparalleled, reminding us of our place in the vast universe.

For those who enjoy water-based activities, many parks offer swimming, kayaking, and fishing opportunities. The Great Smoky Mountains National Park, straddling the border between North Carolina and Tennessee, features pristine mountain streams and rivers where anglers can cast their lines for trout. The park offers cool, refreshing swimming holes and the chance to float down gentle rapids on a lazy summer afternoon.

Birdwatching is a favorite pastime in parks with diverse ecosystems. Acadia National Park is known for its abundant birdlife, including puffins, peregrine falcons, and various songbirds. Bird enthusiasts can explore the park's numerous trails and scenic overlooks, armed with binoculars and field guides, to spot and identify a wide range of feathered friends.

Lastly, many parks offer educational programs and ranger-led activities to enhance visitors' understanding of the natural and cultural aspects of the park. These programs may include guided nature walks, interpretive talks, and interactive exhibits at visitor centers. They provide valuable insights and connect visitors with the passionate individuals who work tirelessly to protect and preserve these special places.

In conclusion, our national and state parks are a treasure trove of activities and attractions catering to various interests and passions. Whether you seek adventure in the great outdoors through hiking and camping, explore these lands' historical and cultural heritage, or simply wish to connect with nature through wildlife observation, stargazing, or water-based activities, the parks offer something for everyone. These protected areas not only showcase the natural beauty of our planet but also provide a means to connect with it on a profound level, fostering a deep appreciation for the wonders of our world and the need to preserve them for future generations.

Wildlife encounters and safety precautions

One of the most exhilarating aspects of spending time in the great outdoors is the opportunity to encounter wildlife in its natural habitat. Whether it's a majestic elk grazing in a meadow, a curious bear exploring a forest, or a colorful bird soaring overhead, these moments can be unforgettable. However, it's crucial to approach wildlife encounters with respect, caution, and a deep understanding of safety precautions. In this section, we will delve into the thrill and responsibility of wildlife encounters, emphasizing the importance of protecting both ourselves and the animals we encounter.

Wildlife encounters can happen unexpectedly, even when we least expect them. National and state parks, forests, and other natural areas are home to various creatures, from the smallest insects to the largest mammals. Yellowstone National Park, for example, is renowned for its abundant wildlife, including bison, wolves, and grizzly bears. Visitors often come to witness these iconic animals in their natural habitat, creating thrilling and sometimes unpredictable encounters.

While the sight of a wild animal can be awe-inspiring, it's essential to remember that these animals are not domesticated pets. They have instincts, behaviors, and territories that must be respected. Approaching too closely or behaving inappropriately around wildlife can have dire consequences for humans and animals.

First and foremost, safety should always be the top priority during wildlife encounters. Keeping a safe distance is crucial to avoid provoking or alarming the animals. Many national parks and wildlife refuges provide guidelines on recommended viewing distances for various species. For instance, it's generally advised to stay at least 100 yards (91 meters) away from bears and wolves in Yellowstone National Park. Observing these guidelines not only protects you but also ensures the well-being of the animals.

It's essential to remain calm and quiet during wildlife encounters. Sudden movements, loud noises, or attempts to approach animals can stress them and lead to unpredictable reactions. This can be particularly dangerous with large mammals like moose or bison, which may perceive humans as threats and charge if they feel cornered or provoked. Wildlife photography should be conducted from a distance with telephoto lenses to avoid causing undue stress to the animals.

Understanding the signs of animal stress or discomfort is crucial for safety. Animals may exhibit signs such as raised fur, vocalizations, agitated behavior, or changes in posture when they feel threatened. If you observe any of these signs, it's imperative to slowly and calmly back away from the animal, giving it the space it needs to relax and return to its natural activities.

Furthermore, it's essential to dispose of food scraps and trash responsibly. Leaving food unattended or littering can attract wildlife to campgrounds and picnic areas, leading to potentially dangerous encounters. Bears, in particular, can become habituated to human food, putting both humans and bears at risk. Following proper food storage and disposal guidelines, such as using bear-proof containers or food lockers, is vital in bear country to prevent these interactions.

Knowledge of local wildlife and their habitats is essential for those exploring areas known for venomous snakes or insects. Wearing appropriate clothing and footwear can reduce the risk of accidental encounters with potentially harmful creatures. When hiking or camping in snake-prone regions, staying on well-marked trails and being aware of your surroundings can help you avoid stepping on a concealed snake.

In marine environments, such as when snorkeling or scuba diving, respecting the marine life and their habitats is paramount. Avoid touching or disturbing coral reefs, which are fragile ecosystems, and refrain from harassing or chasing marine animals. Keeping a respectful distance while observing sea creatures allows for safe and enjoyable encounters without causing harm to these delicate ecosystems.

When engaging in birdwatching or observing nesting sites, it's crucial to use binoculars or spotting scopes to minimize bird disturbance. Nesting birds can be particularly sensitive to human presence, and approaching too closely can lead to the abandonment of nests or harm to chicks.

In conclusion, wildlife encounters in the great outdoors are a privilege and a testament to the beauty and diversity of our natural world. However, with this privilege comes the responsibility to ensure the safety of both humans and the animals we encounter. Respecting recommended viewing distances, remaining calm and quiet, and properly disposing of food and trash are essential safety precautions. Educating oneself about the local wildlife and their behavior is key to fostering safe and respectful interactions. By adhering to these guidelines, we can enjoy the wonders of the wild while protecting the integrity and well-being of the natural world we hold dear.

CHAPTER VI

Making the Most of Your Visit

Tips for avoiding crowds

The allure of the open road, the freedom to explore new destinations, and the comforts of home on wheels make RV travel an increasingly popular choice for adventurers. However, as more people hit the road in recreational vehicles, the challenge of avoiding crowds at popular destinations has become increasingly relevant. Whether you're seeking solitude in nature or simply prefer a more relaxed travel experience, there are strategies you can employ to escape the crowds and make the most of your RV trip. This secion will explore some valuable tips for avoiding crowds on an RV journey, allowing you to savor the tranquility and beauty of less-visited destinations.

One of the most effective ways to avoid crowds is to plan your RV trip during the off-peak season. Popular tourist destinations often experience a surge in visitors during the summer months and major holidays. By opting for shoulder seasons or even winter travel (if you're prepared for cold weather), you can significantly reduce the number of fellow travelers you encounter. Additionally, traveling during off-peak times may offer more flexibility in securing campsite reservations.

Even during peak season, you can reduce crowds by avoiding the most popular days and times. For example, visiting a national park on a weekday rather than a weekend can significantly affect the number of fellow tourists you encounter. Early mornings and late afternoons are also quieter times to explore attractions and hiking trails, as many visitors tend to sleep in or return to their campsites during these hours.

Planning ahead and reserving campsites in advance can be a game-changer in avoiding crowds. Many popular RV campgrounds fill up quickly, so securing your spot ahead of time ensures you won't be left searching for accommodations in a crowded area. Additionally, some campgrounds offer sites that are farther from the main attractions, providing a quieter and more secluded experience.

While famous national parks and tourist hotspots are undoubtedly appealing, lesser-known destinations often offer equally stunning scenery with fewer visitors. Research and explore hidden gems, state parks, national forests, and remote campgrounds that are off the beaten path. These locations can provide a more intimate connection with nature and a sense of discovery that crowded destinations may not offer.

Take advantage of technology to help plan your route and find quieter destinations. Some several apps and websites provide real-time information on campsite availability, including reviews and user ratings. These resources can help you choose less-crowded campgrounds and even provide insights from other RV travelers recently visiting those areas.

Boondocking, also known as dry camping or dispersed camping, involves camping in remote and undeveloped areas without hookups or amenities. While it requires more self-sufficiency and preparedness, it offers the ultimate in solitude and freedom from crowded campgrounds. Many national forests and Bureau of Land Management (BLM) lands permit boondocking, allowing you to enjoy pristine natural settings without the presence of large crowds.

Arriving at your destination on a weekday instead of a weekend can help you secure a quieter spot. Many campers start their weekend trips, leading to busier campgrounds on Fridays and Saturdays. Arriving and departing on weekdays can make a significant difference in the atmosphere of the campsite.

Flexibility is key to avoiding crowds on an RV trip. If you arrive at a destination and find it overcrowded or not to your liking, don't hesitate to adjust your plans and explore nearby alternatives. Sometimes, the best experiences and most beautiful spots are discovered serendipitously when you're open to change.

To preserve the tranquility of less-visited destinations, leaving no trace of your presence is crucial. Follow Leave-No-Trace principles, which include packing out all trash, respecting wildlife and natural habitats, and minimizing noise pollution. By practicing responsible and considerate camping, you help maintain the pristine beauty of these remote areas for future travelers.

In conclusion, RV travel offers a unique blend of adventure and comfort, but the increasing popularity of this mode of travel has led to crowded campgrounds and tourist attractions. To truly savor the serenity and beauty of less-visited destinations, consider traveling during the off-peak season, avoiding peak days and times, reserving campsites in advance, exploring lesser-known destinations, using technology to plan your route, embracing boondocking, planning midweek arrivals and departures, being flexible with your itinerary, and practicing Leave-No-Trace principles. By following these tips and seeking out quieter corners of the world, you can enjoy the peace and solitude that RV travel was meant to provide, making your journey even more rewarding and memorable.

Capturing memories with photography

RV trips are not just about the journey but about the experiences and memories created along the way. In the digital age, photography has become integral to our lives, allowing us to capture and relive those special moments. When you embark on an RV adventure, you have a unique opportunity to document the beauty of the landscapes, the charm of small towns, and the joy of shared experiences. In this section, we will explore the art of capturing memories with photography on an RV trip, from choosing the right gear to mastering composition and storytelling, and how these photographs can become lasting mementos of your journey.

Before hitting the road, selecting the right photography gear for your RV trip is essential. While smartphones have become powerful tools for photography, serious enthusiasts may opt for digital single-lens reflex (DSLR) or mirrorless cameras. These cameras offer greater control over settings, interchangeable lenses, and superior image quality. Regardless of your choice, ensure your gear is in good working condition and that you have all the necessary accessories, such as spare batteries, memory cards, and a sturdy tripod for stable shots. Composition is the foundation of a compelling photograph. It involves arranging elements within the frame to create a visually pleasing and impactful image. While there are various composition techniques, such as the rule of thirds, leading lines, and framing, the key is to find a balance between the elements in your shot. When photographing landscapes, consider foreground interest to add depth, and pay attention to the play of light and shadow to create drama. When capturing people, focus on their expressions and interactions, as these elements can convey the emotions and stories behind the image.

Photography is not just about taking pictures; it's about telling a story. Your RV trip has its narrative, from the excitement of departure to exploring new places and the bonds formed with fellow travelers. Use your camera to document this story, from the scenic highways to the quaint roadside diners and the spontaneous roadside stops. Capture the essence of each location you visit, whether it's the vibrant colors of a bustling market or the serenity of a lakeside campsite. Look for moments that reveal the personalities and connections of your travel companions. These images will become the chapters of your RV adventure.

While the daytime offers its beauty, the night sky unveils a different kind of wonder. Many RV travelers find themselves in remote locations with minimal light pollution, providing an ideal setting for astrophotography. Long exposure shots of starry skies, constellations, and even meteor showers can result in breathtaking photographs. To capture these celestial wonders, you'll need a tripod, a fast lens with a wide aperture, and a camera capable of manual settings. Experiment with different exposure times to find the perfect balance between capturing stars and avoiding overexposure.

Once you've collected a treasure trove of images during your RV trip, the next step is post-processing. Editing software, such as Adobe Lightroom or Photoshop, allows you to enhance your photos' colors, contrast, and sharpness. However, it's crucial to strike a balance between enhancement and maintaining the authenticity of the scene. Remember that editing should complement your storytelling rather than overshadow it. Develop your unique editing style to give your images a consistent and memorable look.

In today's interconnected world, sharing your RV adventure with friends, family, and fellow travelers is easier than ever. Social media platforms like Instagram,

Facebook, and Pinterest provide the perfect canvas to showcase your photography and storytelling skills. Create albums or travel blogs to document your journey, adding captions and anecdotes to give context to your images. Sharing your experiences with others not only creates a sense of community but also inspires and informs fellow RV enthusiasts.

In conclusion, photography is a powerful tool for capturing memories and preserving the essence of your RV trip. By choosing the right gear, mastering composition, telling a story, embracing the golden hour, capturing the night sky, post-processing with care, sharing your journey, and printing and preserving your favorite images, you can create a visual chronicle of your adventure that will bring joy and nostalgia for years to come. Photography not only adds depth to your travel experiences but also allows you to share the beauty and wonder of the world with others, inspiring them to embark on their own RV journeys and create their memories through the lens of a camera.

Connecting with fellow RV travelers

The allure of the open road, the freedom to explore new horizons, and the adventure of the journey—all these elements draw people to the world of RV travel. However, beyond the breathtaking landscapes and picturesque campsites, one of the most enriching aspects of RV life is the opportunity to connect with fellow travelers. RV enthusiasts, often bound by a shared love for the road and a thirst for exploration, form a vibrant and welcoming community on the highways and in campgrounds across the country. In this section, we will delve into the ways in which RV travelers can connect with one another, fostering friendships, sharing experiences, and creating a sense of camaraderie that enhances the RV lifestyle.

The RVing community is a diverse tapestry of travelers, encompassing people from all walks of life and backgrounds. Whether you're a retiree finally embarking on your long-awaited adventures, a young family seeking quality time together, a solo adventurer exploring the unknown, or a digital nomad working remotely from the road, there's a place for you in this inclusive community. This diversity adds depth to the RVing experience, ensuring that there are always new friends to meet and stories to share.

One of the most natural places to connect with fellow RV travelers is at campgrounds and RV parks. These communal spaces serve as hubs for social interaction, where RVers often gather around campfires, picnic tables, or common areas. Striking up a conversation with neighbors is a common and encouraged practice, whether it's a friendly wave across the campsite or an invitation to join in on a shared meal or evening storytelling session.

For those seeking a more structured approach to connecting with fellow RV travelers, numerous RV clubs and associations cater to specific interests and demographics. Groups like the Family Motor Coach Association (FMCA), the Escapees RV Club, and the Good Sam Club provide opportunities for like-minded RVers to meet, attend rallies, and share their knowledge and experiences. These clubs often have chapters or special interest groups focused on various aspects of RV life, such as boondocking, full-time RVing, or vintage RV restoration.

In the digital age, online communities play a significant role in connecting RV travelers. Platforms like RVillage, iRV2, and various RV-focused forums provide spaces for RV enthusiasts to share tips, ask for advice, and plan meet-ups with fellow travelers. These virtual connections can lead to real-life friendships and travel companions as RVers cross paths on the road.

Beyond campgrounds and online communities, RV travelers often have the chance to connect while exploring attractions and destinations. Whether it's striking up a conversation with someone admiring the same scenic view, meeting fellow travelers at a local market, or bonding over a shared hike, the act of exploration itself can lead to unexpected friendships and shared adventures.

One of the most rewarding aspects of connecting with fellow RV travelers is the ability to share experiences. RVers often swap stories of their journeys, recommend must-visit destinations, and offer practical advice on everything from maintenance tips to the best places to find fresh produce on the road. These exchanges of knowledge and experiences not only enhance the RV lifestyle but also foster a sense of community and support.

The RVing community is about friendship, shared experiences, safety, and security. RVers look out for one another, offering assistance in times of need, whether it's helping with a mechanical issue, lending a hand in setting up camp, or providing guidance during severe weather events. This sense of camaraderie and mutual support adds an extra layer of reassurance to life on the road. The

friendships forged on the road often extend beyond the duration of a single trip. Many RV travelers maintain long-lasting connections with fellow enthusiasts, meeting up for future adventures or staying in touch through calls, emails, and social media. These relationships become a cherished part of the RV journey, creating a network of friends scattered across the country.

In the world of RV travel, connecting with fellow travelers is not just an option—it's an integral part of the lifestyle. The shared love for the open road, the thrill of discovery, and the joy of connecting with kindred spirits make RVing more than just a mode of transportation; it's a vibrant and welcoming community that adds depth and richness to the journey. Whether through casual campground conversations, structured RV clubs, online communities, or chance encounters on the road, RV travelers can forge friendships, share experiences, and create lasting memories that enrich their lives and the lives of their fellow wanderers.

Planning for unexpected challenges

Embarking on an RV trip is an exciting adventure that promises freedom, exploration, and the opportunity to create lasting memories. However, it's essential to recognize that the open road can also present unexpected challenges and hurdles that require preparation and adaptability. From mechanical breakdowns to adverse weather conditions, encountering the unexpected is an inherent part of RV travel. This section will explore the importance of planning for unexpected challenges during an RV trip, covering key areas such as vehicle maintenance, emergency preparedness, route flexibility, and maintaining a positive mindset. By taking proactive steps and being ready for the unexpected, RV travelers can ensure a smoother and more enjoyable journey.

Proper vehicle maintenance is the cornerstone of a successful RV trip, as it helps prevent many unexpected challenges. Regularly servicing your RV, including engine checks, tire inspections, and brake maintenance, is crucial. Ensuring that all systems, from plumbing to electrical, are in good working order can prevent inconvenient breakdowns on the road. Prior to departure, perform a comprehensive check to confirm that your RV is roadworthy, and always carry essential spare parts, tools, and a repair manual to address minor issues.

Safety should be a top priority when planning for an RV trip. Prepare an emergency kit that includes essential items such as first aid supplies, fire extinguishers, a flashlight, batteries, and a multipurpose tool. Familiarize yourself with how to use these items effectively. In addition, make sure you have reliable communication devices, such as a cell phone with good coverage and a backup power source, to contact emergency services if needed. Being well-prepared for unforeseen emergencies can significantly affect the outcome of challenging situations.

Mother Nature can present various challenges during an RV trip, from sudden rainstorms to extreme temperatures. Monitoring weather forecasts and being prepared for climate changes is essential. Equip your RV with weather-appropriate gear, such as snow chains or tire covers for winter travel, and awnings or portable fans for hot summer days. Additionally, maintain flexibility in your travel plans to adapt to adverse conditions. Having alternative routes and destinations in mind can help you avoid areas affected by extreme weather and ensure a safer journey.

Thoroughly researching your planned routes and destinations can help you anticipate potential roadblocks and challenges. Use navigation apps and websites that provide up-to-date information on road closures, construction zones, and traffic conditions. It's also wise to check for any travel advisories or restrictions related to the areas you intend to visit. Staying informed allows you to make informed decisions and reroute if necessary, preventing unnecessary stress and delays.

As the popularity of RV travel continues to grow, campgrounds and RV parks can fill up quickly, especially during peak seasons. To avoid unexpected challenges related to accommodation, make reservations well in advance, especially if you plan to stay in popular destinations or during busy times of the year. However, also be prepared for unexpected changes in your plans, and consider having a backup plan for boondocking or finding alternative campsites if your reserved spot becomes unavailable.

While planning and preparation are essential, maintaining a positive mindset is equally crucial when dealing with unexpected challenges. RV travel often involves the thrill of adventure, and with that adventure comes the potential for surprises and setbacks. Embrace these moments as opportunities for personal growth and learning. Approach challenges with patience, adaptability, and a sense of humor. The ability to remain calm and resourceful in the face of the unexpected can turn a potential ordeal into a memorable part of your journey.

The RVing community is a valuable resource for travelers facing unexpected challenges. RVers often form tight-knit bonds and are willing to assist fellow adventurers in times of need. Don't hesitate to seek advice or help from fellow travelers at campgrounds or online forums. Their experiences and insights can provide valuable solutions and guidance, whether it's troubleshooting a technical issue or navigating a challenging route.

In conclusion, RV travel offers a unique blend of freedom, adventure, and discovery. While unexpected challenges may arise, proactive planning, emergency preparedness, route flexibility, thorough research, and a positive mindset can help RV travelers navigate these hurdles confidently and resiliently. Embracing the unpredictable nature of the road is part of what makes RV travel so rewarding. In these moments of challenge and adaptation, travelers often discover the most memorable experiences and stories to share, ultimately adding depth and richness to their RV journeys. Preparedness and a positive attitude are the keys to transforming unexpected challenges into opportunities for growth and adventure on the open road.

CHAPTER VII

Going Green on the Road

Sustainable RV travel practices

The open road's allure and the RV lifestyle's freedom have captured countless travelers' hearts. Yet, as we explore the beauty of our planet, it is essential to consider the impact of our journeys on the environment. Sustainable RV travel practices are becoming increasingly crucial as travelers seek to minimize their ecological footprint while enjoying the wonders of nature. In this section, we will delve into the principles of sustainable RV travel, from responsible camping and energy conservation to waste reduction and preserving natural landscapes. By embracing these practices, RV enthusiasts can enjoy their adventures while protecting the planet for future generations.

One of the core principles of sustainable RV travel is practicing responsible camping, guided by the Leave No Trace ethic. This philosophy emphasizes minimizing our impact on natural environments. RVers can achieve this by staying in designated campgrounds or RV parks, where facilities and services are designed to minimize environmental disruption. When venturing into more remote areas, RV travelers should adhere to guidelines such as camping at least 200 feet away from lakes and streams, respecting wildlife and their habitats, and packing out all trash and waste. By leaving nature as we found it, we preserve its beauty for others to enjoy.

RVs require energy for various purposes, from lighting and appliances to climate control. Sustainable RV travel involves reducing energy consumption and harnessing renewable power sources whenever possible. Installing solar panels on the RV's roof is an increasingly popular option, allowing travelers to generate electricity from sunlight. This reduces reliance on fossil fuels and provides the freedom to camp in off-grid locations while minimizing environmental impact. Additionally, adopting energy-efficient appliances, LED lighting, and programmable thermostats can further decrease energy usage.

Water is a precious resource, and practicing water conservation is a vital component of sustainable RV travel. RVers should be mindful of their water usage, take shorter showers, fix leaks promptly, and use low-flow faucets and showerheads. Collecting rainwater for non-potable uses, such as flushing toilets or washing dishes, is another sustainable practice. Additionally, choosing campgrounds with water-saving amenities, such as waterless or composting toilets, helps reduce the environmental impact of RV travel.

Minimizing waste production and embracing recycling practices are essential aspects of sustainable RV travel. RV travelers should carry reusable containers for food storage and opt for products with minimal packaging. Recycling bins are available at many campgrounds and RV parks, making it convenient to dispose of recyclable materials properly. Moreover, composting organic waste, such as food scraps, not only reduces landfill contributions but also enriches the soil when disposed of in suitable locations.

Efficient travel planning can significantly reduce carbon emissions associated with RV travel. Consider planning routes that minimize travel distances, reduce fuel consumption, and avoid congested areas. Slower driving speeds and the use of cruise control can also improve fuel efficiency. Moreover, embracing a relaxed travel pace reduces emissions and allows travelers to savor the journey and immerse themselves in local communities and natural landscapes.

Choosing sustainable products and supporting eco-conscious businesses can make a significant difference in the environmental impact of RV travel. Seek out campgrounds and RV parks that have adopted sustainable practices, such as using renewable energy sources or implementing water-saving measures. Purchase eco-friendly RV accessories and cleaning products to reduce the release of harmful chemicals into the environment. Supporting local and sustainable businesses along your route also fosters responsible tourism and helps protect the natural and cultural heritage of the places you visit.

As responsible RV travelers, it is our duty not only to practice sustainable travel but also to educate and advocate for its importance within our community. Share your knowledge and experiences with fellow RV enthusiasts, encouraging them to embrace sustainable practices. Participate in local clean-up efforts and conservation projects during your travels. Engage with campground owners and local authorities to promote sustainability and responsible tourism. By spreading awareness and fostering a culture of sustainability, we can collectively minimize the ecological impact of RV travel.

Sustainable RV travel practices are a vital step toward ensuring that the beauty and wonder of our planet remain accessible for generations to come. Responsible camping, energy conservation, water conservation, waste reduction, efficient travel planning, supporting sustainable businesses, and educating and advocating for sustainability are all essential elements of this journey. RV enthusiasts have the unique opportunity to explore the world while treading lightly upon it. By embracing sustainable travel practices, we can protect the environment, minimize our ecological footprint, and contribute to a brighter and more sustainable future for ourselves and future generations of RV travelers.

Reducing your environmental footprint

RV camping allows us to immerse ourselves in the beauty of the great outdoors while enjoying the comforts of home on wheels. However, with the joys of RV travel come environmental responsibilities. As stewards of the environment, minimizing our impact on nature and adopting sustainable practices while camping in our recreational vehicles is crucial. In this section, we will explore ways to reduce your environmental footprint during RV camping, from conserving resources like water and energy to practicing responsible waste management and respecting the natural surroundings. By embracing these principles, RV enthusiasts can enjoy nature responsibly and contribute to preserving our planet.

Resource conservation is fundamental to reducing your environmental footprint during RV camping. Water is a precious resource, so use it wisely. Take shorter showers, fix leaks promptly, and consider using a high-efficiency, low-flow showerhead. Use a bucket to collect water while waiting for it to heat up, and repurpose this greywater for flushing toilets or watering plants. Energy efficiency is equally important. Installing solar panels on your RV can provide a sustainable source of electricity, reducing the need for fossil fuels. Use LED lighting and energy-efficient appliances to minimize energy consumption. Turn off lights and devices when not in use, and unplug chargers to prevent vampire power drain. A programmable thermostat can help regulate indoor temperatures, saving energy while keeping you comfortable.

Minimizing waste is another crucial aspect of reducing your environmental impact during RV camping. Carry reusable containers for food storage and opt for products with minimal packaging to reduce single-use plastics.

Avoid disposable dishes and utensils by using reusable alternatives. Composting organic waste, such as food scraps, can significantly reduce the amount of trash generated. When disposing of waste, follow campground recycling guidelines and ensure that recyclables are properly separated from general trash.

Practicing responsible camping is a core principle of reducing your environmental footprint. The Leave No Trace ethic emphasizes minimizing your impact on natural environments. Stay in designated campgrounds or RV parks whenever possible, as these areas have facilities that help minimize environmental disruption. When camping in more remote locations, adhere to guidelines such as camping at least 200 feet away from lakes and streams, respecting wildlife and their habitats, and packing out all trash and waste. By leaving nature as you found it, you contribute to preserving pristine landscapes.

As responsible RV campers, educating and advocating for sustainable practices within the RV community is essential. Share your knowledge and experiences with fellow enthusiasts, encouraging them to embrace eco-friendly habits. Engage in local clean-up efforts and conservation projects during your travels to give back to the communities and environments you visit. Support campgrounds and organizations that prioritize sustainability and responsible tourism. By actively participating in these efforts, you help raise awareness and promote a culture of environmental responsibility among RV travelers.

Respecting wildlife and natural surroundings is integral to reducing your environmental footprint. Observe wildlife from a distance, refraining from feeding or approaching animals. Use binoculars and cameras with telephoto lenses to capture images without disturbing wildlife. Avoid loud noises and excessive human activity in sensitive ecosystems. Stay on designated trails and avoid trampling on fragile vegetation. Stick to established paths to minimize soil erosion and habitat disruption when enjoying outdoor activities such as hiking or biking.

Consider investing in eco-friendly RV accessories to reduce your environmental impact further. Choose biodegradable cleaning products that are safe for the environment. Use solar-powered outdoor lighting and portable solar chargers for your devices. Opt for camping gear made from sustainable materials, such as bamboo or recycled plastics. By making conscious choices in your products, you can reduce your overall environmental impact.

Reducing your environmental footprint during RV camping is not just a matter of personal responsibility; it's a collective effort to preserve the natural beauty of our planet. Resource conservation, waste reduction, responsible camping, community engagement, wildlife respect, and eco-friendly accessories are all crucial elements of this endeavor. By embracing these practices, RV enthusiasts can enjoy the wonders of nature while contributing to the well-being of the environment. Responsible RV camping is not only about experiencing the great outdoors—it's about leaving a positive legacy for future generations of RV travelers, ensuring that they, too, can revel in the beauty of our natural world.

Responsible camping and waste disposal

Embarking on an RV trip is an exciting adventure filled with the promise of exploration and outdoor experiences. Yet, with this freedom and mobility comes the responsibility to minimize our environmental impact. Responsible camping and proper waste disposal are essential aspects of this responsibility, ensuring that we leave nature as pristine as we found it and safeguard the environment for future generations. In this section, we will delve into responsible camping and waste disposal principles during an RV trip, covering areas such as campground etiquette, graywater and blackwater management, recycling, and minimizing waste. By adopting these practices, RV travelers can enjoy their journey while preserving the beauty of the landscapes they traverse.

Responsible camping begins with adhering to the Leave No Trace principles, which emphasize minimizing our impact on natural environments. When staying in campgrounds or RV parks, following campground rules and guidelines is crucial. These areas are equipped with facilities designed to minimize environmental disruption. Campers should stay within designated campsites, respect boundaries, and not encroach on vegetation. Avoid making new fire rings or clearing additional spaces for tents. Follow campground quiet hours and respect the peace and privacy of fellow campers.

Managing graywater and blackwater from your RV is vital to responsible camping. Graywater consists of wastewater generated from sinks, showers, and washing machines, while blackwater is sewage from toilets. It's essential to use appropriate disposal facilities for these types of waste provided by campgrounds or RV parks. Never dump graywater or blackwater on the ground, as it can contaminate water sources and harm the environment. Many campgrounds have designated dumping stations equipped with sewage and graywater disposal facilities for RVs.

Minimizing waste and practicing recycling is another key component of responsible camping. Carry reusable containers for food storage and opt for products with minimal packaging to reduce single-use plastics. Use reusable dishware and utensils to avoid disposable options. Most campgrounds and RV parks offer recycling bins, making it convenient to dispose of recyclable materials properly. Separate recyclables from general trash and follow the recycling guidelines specific to the campground. Embrace the "reduce, reuse, and recycle" principles to minimize waste generation.

Conscious choices and thoughtful planning can significantly reduce waste during an RV trip. Before departure, carefully consider the items you bring, focusing on necessity rather than convenience. Opt for bulk purchases to reduce excess packaging, and carry reusable shopping bags. Use a water filtration system or refillable water containers instead of buying bottled water. Plan meals to minimize food waste, and store leftovers in airtight containers for later consumption. These measures allow RV travelers to minimize the amount of trash generated during their journey.

Proper disposal of hazardous waste, such as propane canisters, batteries, and chemicals, is crucial for responsible camping. These items should never be thrown in regular trash bins or left behind in the wilderness. Many campgrounds and RV parks have designated areas or programs for the safe disposal of hazardous materials. Research the waste disposal guidelines specific to your location and make use of these facilities. Additionally, consider using rechargeable batteries to reduce the number of disposable batteries used during your trip.

The overarching principle of responsible camping is to leave nature as you found it. This means avoiding any alterations to the natural environment. Do not dig trenches around your campsite or cut down trees or vegetation. Respect wildlife by observing animals from a distance, refraining from feeding them, and using telephoto lenses for photography. Stay on designated trails to minimize soil erosion and habitat disruption when hiking or biking. The goal is to enjoy nature's beauty without leaving a trace of your presence.

As responsible RV campers, spreading awareness of responsible camping practices within the RV community and beyond is essential. Share your knowledge and experiences with fellow travelers, encouraging them to adopt eco-friendly habits. Participate in local clean-up efforts and conservation projects during your travels to give back to the communities and environments you visit. Engage with campground owners and local authorities to promote sustainability and responsible tourism. By actively participating in these efforts, you help raise awareness and promote a culture of environmental responsibility among RV travelers.

Responsible camping and waste disposal during an RV trip are not just matters of personal responsibility; they are essential steps toward preserving the natural beauty of our planet. Whether you are staying in a campground, an RV park, or a remote wilderness area, Leave No Trace principles, proper graywater and blackwater management, recycling, waste reduction, and conscientious choices all contribute to responsible camping. By adopting these practices, RV travelers can enjoy the great outdoors while leaving a positive legacy for future generations. Responsible camping is not only about the journey—it's about ensuring that the remarkable landscapes and environments we explore remain unspoiled and thriving for years to come.

Supporting conservation efforts within national parks

Embarking on an RV trip is an exciting journey into the heart of nature, where majestic national parks await exploration. These protected areas represent the epitome of our natural heritage, rich in biodiversity and scenic splendor. However, the privilege of visiting these national treasures carries with it the duty to become stewards of the environment and support conservation efforts. Responsible camping, volunteering, financial contributions, educational engagement, respect for wildlife and natural landscapes, promoting sustainable practices, and leading by example are all integral facets of supporting conservation within national parks during an RV trip.

Responsible camping is the cornerstone of supporting conservation within national parks. The Leave No Trace ethic underscores the importance of minimizing our impact on natural environments. RV travelers should adhere to campground rules and guidelines, staying within designated campsites to avoid encroaching on vegetation. In remote areas, camping at least 200 feet away from lakes and streams, respecting wildlife and their habitats, and carrying out all trash and waste are essential practices. By leaving nature as pristine as we found it, we help protect the ecological balance of these special places.

Volunteering is an active and hands-on way to support conservation efforts within national parks. Many parks offer volunteer programs that enable RV travelers to participate in activities such as trail maintenance, habitat restoration, wildlife monitoring, and educational outreach. Volunteering contributes to the park's well-being and fosters a deeper connection to the natural world. It allows RV travelers to become part of the solution, working alongside dedicated conservationists to preserve the park's ecological integrity.

Financial contributions play a crucial role in funding conservation initiatives within national parks. RV travelers can directly donate to park-specific projects or support nonprofit organizations committed to park conservation. National parks often have foundations or associations dedicated to raising funds for essential projects, such as habitat restoration and educational programs. Contributions from RV travelers help ensure the long-term sustainability of these vital initiatives.

Educational engagement is another potent tool for supporting conservation. RV travelers can share their experiences and knowledge with fellow travelers and park visitors, emphasizing responsible behavior and the importance of preserving these unique ecosystems. By raising awareness about conservation issues within national parks, RV travelers become advocates for positive change, inspiring others to respect park rules and guidelines and embrace a sense of responsibility toward these natural wonders.

Respect for wildlife and natural landscapes is fundamental to conservation efforts. RV travelers should observe wildlife from a distance, avoiding the temptation to feed or approach animals. Using binoculars and cameras with telephoto lenses allows for close observation without disturbing wildlife. Avoiding loud noises and excessive human activity in sensitive ecosystems is essential. Staying on designated trails when hiking or exploring minimizes soil erosion and habitat disruption, contributing to the overall health of the park's ecosystem.

Promoting sustainable practices and leading by example within the RV community is vital to conservation support. RV travelers can encourage fellow enthusiasts to adopt eco-friendly habits such as responsible camping, waste reduction, and resource conservation. Engaging in local clean-up efforts and conservation projects during travels actively contributes to the park's and surrounding communities' well-being. Collaboration with park rangers and staff to learn about ongoing conservation initiatives and opportunities for involvement can further strengthen the commitment to conservation.

In conclusion, supporting conservation efforts within national parks during an RV trip is both a responsibility and a privilege. These natural wonders provide us with unparalleled beauty and ecological significance, and we must ensure their preservation. Responsible camping, volunteering, financial contributions, educational engagement, respect for wildlife and natural landscapes, promoting sustainable practices, and leading by example are all essential aspects of this commitment. RV travelers have the unique opportunity to experience and protect these remarkable landscapes, ensuring they remain thriving and intact for generations to come.

CHAPTER VIII

The RV Lifestyle and Community

The sense of community among RV travelers

In today's fast-paced world, the concept of community has undergone a transformation. Gone are the days when it was primarily associated with geographical proximity. Instead, a new form of community has emerged among RV travelers, transcending physical boundaries and fostering connections based on shared interests and lifestyles. The sense of community among RV travelers is a unique and vibrant phenomenon, driven by the desire for adventure, freedom, and a deeper connection with fellow enthusiasts. This section explores this evolving community's various facets, significance, and factors that contribute to its growth and strength.

RV travelers, often called "nomads on wheels," embark on journeys that take them across vast landscapes, exploring new territories and cultures. These travelers come from diverse backgrounds, ages, and walks of life. What unites them is a common love for adventure and the freedom to roam. The shared experiences of navigating the open road, discovering hidden gems, and facing life's challenges on the move create a powerful bond among RV enthusiasts. This shared journey forms the foundation of the sense of community within this group.

One key element that strengthens the RV traveler community is the genuine desire to connect with others. In an era marked by increasing digitalization and social isolation, RV travelers embrace face-to-face interactions and value the relationships they form along the way.

Campgrounds and RV parks serve as hubs for socializing and provide opportunities for travelers to come together, exchange stories, and offer assistance when needed. The camaraderie that develops among these individuals is a testament to the authenticity of their connections.

Moreover, the sense of community among RV travelers is built on mutual support and a willingness to help one another. Whether it's sharing tips on finding the best boondocking spots, assisting with technical issues, or lending a hand in emergencies, RV enthusiasts demonstrate a strong sense of solidarity. The RV lifestyle often presents challenges, such as maintenance problems or unexpected breakdowns, and having a community of like-minded individuals who can offer advice or lend a hand is invaluable.

Another factor contributing to the sense of community among RV travelers is the shared appreciation for the beauty of nature and the outdoors. RV enthusiasts deeply respect the environment and often engage in activities like hiking, fishing, or wildlife observation. This shared love for nature creates a bond that goes beyond the confines of traditional community boundaries. Together, they work towards preserving the natural beauty of the places they visit, promoting sustainable practices, and leaving minimal ecological footprints.

Furthermore, technology has played a pivotal role in fostering and sustaining the RV traveler community. Social media platforms and online forums have become virtual meeting places for RV enthusiasts, allowing them to connect, share experiences, and seek advice from a global network of fellow travelers. These digital spaces facilitate the exchange of information, the planning of meetups, and the formation of long-lasting friendships, transcending geographical limitations.

The sense of community among RV travelers is not limited to the road; it extends into the broader context of lifestyle choices and values. Many RV enthusiasts are drawn to this way of life as a means to escape the consumer-driven culture that dominates modern society. They prioritize experiences over possessions, minimalism over materialism, and freedom over the constraints of traditional living. This shared set of values creates a sense of belonging and purpose within the community, as they support and inspire one another to live life on their own terms.

In conclusion, the sense of community among RV travelers is a testament to the power of shared experiences, values, and lifestyles. It is a vibrant and evolving phenomenon that transcends physical boundaries and fosters connections among individuals who are bound by their love for adventure, nature, and the freedom to roam. The RV traveler community is characterized by genuine interactions, mutual support, and a shared commitment to preserving the environment. In a world where digital connections often replace face-to-face relationships, this community stands as a shining example of the enduring human need for connection and community, even in the most unconventional of settings. As RV travelers continue to explore the open road and build meaningful relationships, their sense of community only grows stronger, reminding them of the beauty of human connection and the pursuit of a less ordinary life.

Personal stories and experiences from RV enthusiasts

The world of RV enthusiasts is a vibrant and diverse one, comprised of individuals who have embraced a unique way of life centered around the open road, adventure, and the freedom to explore. While RVs may vary in size and style, the common thread uniting this community is their passion for travel and the stories and experiences they accumulate. In this section, we delve into the personal narratives of RV enthusiasts, sharing their tales of adventure, self-discovery, and the lessons learned from life on the road.

For many RV enthusiasts, the decision to embark on a life of travel is driven by a desire for adventure and a longing to break free from the constraints of a conventional lifestyle. One such individual is Sarah, who left behind a stable job and the familiar comforts of home to pursue a nomadic existence in her RV. She recounts the exhilaration of her first solo cross-country trip, where every new town and scenic vista offered a fresh sense of wonder. Sarah's story underscores the transformative power of adventure, demonstrating how the RV lifestyle can awaken a sense of curiosity and exploration that lies dormant within us.

The road less traveled often leads to unexpected encounters and friendships that enrich the lives of RV enthusiasts. John and Lisa, a retired couple from Oregon, share the heartwarming story of a chance meeting with fellow travelers at a remote campsite. What began as a simple exchange of pleasantries over a campfire became a lasting friendship. Over the years, they have shared countless meals, campfires, and travel tips, creating a bond that transcends the limitations of age and background. John and Lisa's experience highlights the capacity of the RV lifestyle to forge connections with kindred spirits and create a sense of community wherever the road may lead.

In addition to the joy of making new friends, RV enthusiasts often find solace and inspiration in the serenity of natural landscapes. Emily, a solo traveler with a passion for photography, describes her journey through the national parks of the American West as a source of profound self-discovery. Amidst the towering red rock formations and tranquil desert sunsets, she found a sense of inner peace and a renewed appreciation for the beauty of the natural world. Emily's story underscores the therapeutic and contemplative aspects of RV travel, reminding us of the healing power of nature.

The RV lifestyle also offers opportunities for personal growth and self-sufficiency. Mark, a former corporate executive, left behind his high-powered career to embrace a simpler life on the road. He reflects on the challenges and rewards of learning to repair and maintain his RV, as well as the satisfaction of living a more sustainable and eco-conscious lifestyle. Mark's journey serves as a testament to the transformative potential of RV living, showing how it can lead to a greater sense of self-reliance and fulfillment.

While RV travel is often associated with freedom and spontaneity, it also requires careful planning and adaptability. Karen and Mike, a couple who have been RVing for over a decade, share their experience of weathering unexpected storms and mechanical breakdowns. These challenges, they say, have taught them valuable lessons in resilience and resourcefulness. Karen and Mike's story reminds us that the road may not always be smooth, but it is the ability to overcome obstacles that defines the character of an RV enthusiast.

The RV lifestyle can also be a means of giving back to communities and making a positive impact. Linda and Robert, a retired couple with a deep sense of social responsibility, have used their RV to volunteer in disaster-stricken areas and assist in relief efforts. They recount the fulfillment they derive from using their skills and resources to help others during times of crisis. Linda and Robert's story demonstrates that RV enthusiasts often find creative ways to contribute to society while pursuing their passion for travel.

In conclusion, the personal stories and experiences of RV enthusiasts are a testament to the richness and diversity of this unique way of life. Whether driven by a thirst for adventure, a longing for connection, a desire for self-discovery, or a commitment to making a difference, RV enthusiasts share a common love for the open road and the experiences it brings. Their narratives remind us that life on the road is not just about the places visited but also the people met, the lessons learned, and the personal growth achieved. As the RV community continues to grow and evolve, it serves as a source of inspiration for those seeking a less ordinary life, where the journey becomes the destination.

RV clubs and organizations

In the world of recreational vehicle (RV) enthusiasts, a sense of community is not just a byproduct of the lifestyle; it is actively nurtured and enhanced through the countless RV clubs and organizations that bring like- minded individuals together. These clubs serve as camaraderie, knowledge sharing, and support hubs, allowing RV enthusiasts to connect with others who share their passion for adventure and the open road. In this section, we explore the significance of RV clubs and organizations, their diverse offerings, and their role in enriching the RVing experience.

RV clubs and organizations vary in size, scope, and focus, catering to a wide range of interests and preferences within the RV community. One of the most well-known and established clubs is the Good Sam Club, which boasts millions of members across North America. Founded in 1966, the Good Sam Club offers a host of benefits, including discounts on campgrounds, fuel, and RV products. Moreover, it provides a platform for members to connect through local chapters, regional rallies, and national events, fostering a sense of belonging and a shared identity among RV enthusiasts.

Similarly, the Escapees RV Club, founded in 1978, focuses on providing resources and support to full-time RVers. It offers services such as mail forwarding, job boards, and

RV education, catering to the unique needs of those who have chosen the RV lifestyle as their primary mode of living. Escapees also operates a network of RV parks and co-op parks where members can find a welcoming community of fellow travelers.

For those interested in the social aspects of RVing, there are clubs like the Family Motor Coach Association (FMCA) and the Wally Byam Caravan Club International (WBCCI). The FMCA, established in 1963, is open to all types of RVers and organizes national conventions with seminars, entertainment, and a strong emphasis on camaraderie. On the other hand, the WBCCI, founded by the creator of Airstream trailers, focuses exclusively on Airstream owners, fostering a close-knit community centered around this iconic brand.

Beyond these nationally recognized clubs, countless other RV organizations cater to specific niches and interests within the RV community. For example, the Loners on Wheels club is designed for solo RV travelers, providing a supportive network for those who may be exploring the open road alone. The Vintage Airstream Club celebrates the restoration and preservation of vintage Airstream trailers, bringing together enthusiasts who share a love for the classic aluminum design. These niche clubs offer specialized knowledge, events, and connections tailored to the unique interests of their members.

RV clubs and organizations serve various essential functions within the RV community. First and foremost, they provide a sense of belonging and camaraderie. Many RVers find comfort in knowing that there is a network of like-minded individuals who share their passion for travel and adventure. Whether through local chapter meetings, regional rallies, or national conventions, these clubs create opportunities for RV enthusiasts to come together, form friendships, and exchange stories and experiences.

Education and information sharing are also significant aspects of RV clubs. Most organizations offer educational resources, workshops, and seminars on topics ranging from RV maintenance and safety to travel planning and destination recommendations. This wealth of knowledge helps RVers become more confident and informed travelers, enabling them to enjoy their adventures to the fullest while minimizing potential pitfalls.

Furthermore, RV clubs often negotiate discounts and special deals with campgrounds, RV parks, and suppliers, translating into tangible benefits for their members. These savings on camping fees, fuel, and RV-related products can offset the club membership cost, making it a financially wise choice for many RV enthusiasts. Another vital function of RV clubs is advocacy and representation. Many organizations actively engage in advocating for the rights and interests of RVers, both legislatively and within the RV industry. They work to ensure that RVers have access to safe and enjoyable travel experiences and that their voices are heard in matters that affect the RVing community.

Lastly, RV clubs and organizations often give back to society through charitable initiatives and community service projects. Many RVers have a strong sense of social responsibility and use their shared passion for travel to impact the communities they visit positively. Clubs may organize charity drives, volunteer opportunities, or disaster relief efforts, reinforcing the idea that RVing is not just about self-indulgence but also about giving back.

In conclusion, RV clubs and organizations play a significant role in the lives of RV enthusiasts, enhancing their experience on the open road and fostering a sense of community and camaraderie. These clubs cater to diverse interests, providing valuable resources, education, and support. Whether through social gatherings, educational seminars, or advocacy efforts, RV clubs enrich the RVing lifestyle and underscore the idea that the journey is as much about the people you meet along the way as it is about the destinations you visit. In the ever-expanding world of RVing, these clubs continue to thrive, creating bonds among travelers and enriching the lives of those who call the open road their home.

How the RV lifestyle can enrich your life

The RV lifestyle, often associated with freedom, adventure, and a deep connection to the open road, has captured the imaginations of many. Beyond its surface appeal, however, lies a transformative way of life that can profoundly enrich one's life in various ways. This section explores how the RV lifestyle can bring about personal growth, strengthen relationships, foster a deeper connection with nature, and promote a sense of freedom and self-discovery.

One of the most compelling aspects of the RV lifestyle is its potential for personal growth. Living life on the road requires adaptability, problem-solving skills, and a willingness to step outside one's comfort zone. RV enthusiasts often face unexpected challenges, whether navigating unfamiliar terrain, managing limited resources, or learning the intricacies of RV maintenance. These challenges, while demanding, offer valuable opportunities for self-improvement. RVers learn to become more self-reliant, resourceful, and resilient as they overcome obstacles and acquire new skills. The sense of accomplishment that comes from successfully tackling these challenges can boost self-confidence and contribute to personal growth.

Furthermore, the RV lifestyle encourages individuals to embrace minimalism and simplicity. With limited space in their RVs, RVers must carefully consider the items they carry with them, prioritizing the essentials and shedding excess baggage. This shift towards a minimalist mindset can lead to a deeper appreciation for what truly matters in life. RVers often find that they can live with less and that the pursuit of material possessions loses its grip on their happiness. This newfound simplicity can lead to a sense of contentment and liberation from consumerism, enriching one's life by emphasizing experiences over possessions.

The RV lifestyle also has the power to strengthen relationships, whether it's with family, friends, or even new acquaintances. Many RVers choose to travel with loved ones, creating opportunities for quality time spent together. Family trips in an RV can promote bonding and create cherished memories that last a lifetime. Moreover, the close quarters of an RV often encourage open communication and cooperation among family members, fostering stronger relationships. For retirees, the RV lifestyle offers the chance to reconnect with their partner and rediscover shared interests, leading to a more fulfilling retirement.

Beyond family, RVers often find a sense of community on the road. Campgrounds and RV parks serve as social hubs where travelers come together, swap stories, and form connections with fellow enthusiasts. The RV community is known for its hospitality and willingness to help one another, whether it's offering travel advice, lending a hand with technical issues, or sharing a campfire and a meal. These connections, born out of a shared passion for RVing, can lead to lasting friendships that enrich one's life with a sense of belonging and support.

The RV lifestyle also nurtures a deeper connection with nature, a facet that resonates strongly with many enthusiasts. RVers can immerse themselves in breathtaking natural landscapes, from national parks' rugged beauty to secluded campgrounds' serenity. The freedom to choose their surroundings fosters a sense of wonder and appreciation for the world's natural wonders.

RVers often engage in outdoor activities like hiking, biking, fishing, and wildlife observation, forging a profound connection with the environment. This connection can lead to a heightened awareness of conservation and a commitment to preserving the natural beauty of the places they visit, ultimately enriching one's life by fostering a deeper connection with the planet.

Moreover, the RV lifestyle offers a unique opportunity for self-discovery and the pursuit of personal passions. Many RVers use their time on the road to explore new hobbies, interests, and creative pursuits. Whether it's writing, painting, photography, or simply taking the time to read and reflect, the RV lifestyle encourages individuals to prioritize their passions and invest in activities that bring them joy. This self-discovery can lead to a more fulfilling and purpose-driven life.

Perhaps one of the most profound ways the RV lifestyle enriches one's life is by promoting a sense of freedom. The ability to pick up and go whenever and wherever one desires is a liberating experience. RVers are not bound by the constraints of a fixed location, and this freedom allows them to follow their whims, explore new horizons, and live life on their own terms. This sense of autonomy and self-determination can lead to a renewed zest for life, as RVers embrace the adventure of each new day.

In conclusion, the RV lifestyle has the potential to enrich one's life in multifaceted ways. It fosters personal growth, encourages simplicity and minimalism, strengthens relationships, nurtures a deeper connection with nature, and promotes a sense of freedom and self-discovery. Whether it's the thrill of overcoming challenges on the road, the joy of shared adventures with loved ones, or the sense of wonder inspired by natural beauty, the RV lifestyle offers a unique and transformative way of life that has the power to enhance the quality and depth of one's existence. As more individuals are drawn to the open road and the possibilities it holds, the RV lifestyle continues to prove that the journey itself is an enriching and rewarding destination.

CHAPTER IX

Returning Home and Reflection

Dealing with post-trip blues

The end of an RV trip often brings mixed emotions. While the memories of adventure, scenic vistas, and quality time spent with loved ones linger, there can also be a sense of melancholy known as post-trip blues. This phenomenon, akin to the post-vacation blues, occurs when the reality of returning to everyday life sets in after the excitement of an RV journey. In this section, we will explore the causes of post-trip blues, their emotional impact, and practical coping strategies for overcoming this temporary but common feeling.

Post-trip blues can be attributed to several factors, each contributing to the overall sense of sadness or unease. Firstly, the stark contrast between RV travel's freedom and novelty and daily life's routine and responsibilities can be jarring. The shift from constantly changing scenery, new experiences, and adventure to the familiar routine of work, chores, and obligations can lead to a sense of monotony and dissatisfaction. This stark contrast between the excitement of the journey and the mundanity of home life can trigger post-trip blues.

Secondly, the bonds and connections formed during an RV trip, whether with family, friends, or fellow travelers, can be significant. The shared experiences, inside jokes, and the simple joy of being together in a confined space create a unique sense of togetherness and camaraderie. Returning to separate lives and physical distances can lead to feelings of loneliness and a longing for the close-knit community forged on the road.

Additionally, the stimulation and sensory overload experienced during RV travel can lead to heightened excitement and engagement. The constant exposure to new sights, sounds, and sensations can create a natural high that is difficult to replicate in daily life's more controlled and predictable environment. This contrast in sensory experiences can leave individuals feeling underwhelmed or even emotionally flat when they return home.

Moreover, the anticipation and planning of an RV trip can be a source of excitement. The months or weeks leading up to the journey are often filled with research, itinerary planning, and anticipation. When the trip ends, this sense of anticipation is abruptly replaced by a void, leaving individuals without a clear sense of purpose or a goal to work toward.

The emotional impact of post-trip blues can vary from mild to severe, depending on the individual and the nature of the trip. Some may experience a sense of restlessness, finding it challenging to settle back into their daily routines and yearning for the open road. Others may feel a more profound sadness, struggling with the loss of the freedom and adventure they experienced while RVing. It's not uncommon for individuals to feel a sense of nostalgia, reminiscing about the trip and longing to relive those moments.

However, there are practical strategies for coping with post-trip blues and transitioning back to everyday life more smoothly. First and foremost, it's essential to acknowledge and accept the feelings of sadness or melancholy. These emotions are a natural part of the post-trip experience and should not be dismissed. By acknowledging these feelings, individuals can begin the process of healing and moving forward.

One effective way to cope with post-trip blues is to create a post-trip routine. This routine can help bridge the gap between RV travel's excitement and daily life's structure. Incorporating elements from the trip, such as regular outdoor activities, travel-themed hobbies, or even planning the next adventure, can provide a sense of continuity and purpose.

Another strategy is to maintain connections with the people met during the trip. Technology has made it easier than ever to stay in touch with fellow travelers, whether through social media, online forums, or group chats. These connections can provide a sense of ongoing community and support, helping to alleviate feelings of loneliness.

Additionally, sharing and preserving memories from the RV journey can be therapeutic. Creating a travel journal, scrapbook, or digital photo album can help individuals relive the trip's highlights and keep the memories alive. Sharing these memories with friends and family can also foster a sense of connection and allow loved ones to be a part of the journey even after it ends.

Engaging in self-care and practicing mindfulness can be beneficial as well. Activities such as meditation, yoga, or simply spending time in nature can help individuals recenter themselves and reduce stress. Practicing gratitude by reflecting on the positive aspects of the trip and the lessons learned can also contribute to a more positive outlook.

Lastly, planning for the future can help individuals combat post-trip blues. Setting new goals, whether they are related to travel or personal development, can provide a sense of purpose and excitement for what lies ahead. The act of planning and looking forward to future adventures can help ease the transition back to daily life.

In conclusion, post-trip blues are a common and understandable emotional response to the end of an RV journey. The contrast between the excitement of travel and the routine of daily life, the bonds formed on the road, and the sensory overload experienced during the trip can all contribute to these feelings of sadness or unease. However, with acknowledgment, self-care, and implementing practical coping strategies, individuals can navigate through this adjustment period and even use it as an opportunity for personal growth and reflection. Ultimately, the RV lifestyle offers a wealth of experiences and memories that can enrich one's life long after the trip ends.

The lasting impact of national park exploration

National parks have long been celebrated as natural beauty, biodiversity, and cultural significance sanctuaries. These protected areas, set aside for the enjoyment and preservation of their unique landscapes and ecosystems, hold a special place in nature enthusiasts and adventurers' hearts. The exploration of national parks has a profound and lasting impact on individuals, communities, and society as a whole. In this section, we will delve into how national park exploration leaves an enduring mark on the lives of those who visit them and the world at large.

First and foremost, exploring national parks fosters a

deep appreciation for the natural world. These pristine landscapes, ranging from the towering peaks of the Rocky Mountains to the lush forests of the Amazon, serve as living classrooms where visitors can witness the wonders of nature up close. The sight of a majestic waterfall, the sound of a rushing river, or the scent of blooming wildflowers can awaken the senses and instill a profound respect for the Earth's beauty and complexity. National park exploration encourages individuals to connect with the environment and recognize the importance of preserving it for future generations.

Moreover, national parks provide invaluable opportunities for education and learning. Interpretive centers, ranger-led programs, and guided tours offer visitors a chance to delve into these protected areas' history, geology, and ecology. These educational experiences deepen one's understanding of the natural world and ignite a passion for lifelong learning. Inspired by their experiences in national parks, many individuals become advocates for environmental conservation and stewards of our planet's fragile ecosystems.

National park exploration has a transformative effect on personal well-being and mental health. Time spent in these natural sanctuaries allows individuals to disconnect from the pressures of modern life, reduce stress, and find solace in the serenity of the great outdoors. Studies have shown that exposure to natural environments can lower blood pressure, boost mood, and enhance cognitive function. The therapeutic benefits of spending time in national parks are widely recognized, and many people turn to these natural havens as a means of rejuvenation and self-care.

Furthermore, national park exploration fosters a sense of adventure and curiosity. These protected areas offer endless activities, from hiking and camping to wildlife watching and photography. The sense of discovery that comes with exploring new trails, spotting elusive wildlife, or uncovering hidden gems within the park fuels a spirit of exploration that often extends beyond the park boundaries. National park enthusiasts often become avid travelers and seekers of new experiences, broadening their horizons and embracing the thrill of adventure in other aspects of their lives.

The economic impact of national park exploration is also significant. These protected areas draw millions of visitors each year, contributing billions of dollars to local economies. The tourism industry that thrives around national parks generates jobs, supports local businesses, and stimulates economic growth in nearby communities. The revenue generated from park visitation often funds conservation efforts, infrastructure improvements, and educational programs, ensuring the continued preservation and accessibility of these natural treasures.

Moreover, national park exploration plays a pivotal role in preserving and protecting natural and cultural heritage. The designation of a national park often involves a rigorous process of assessing the area's ecological significance and historical value. Once designated, national parks receive legal protection and management to safeguard their unique attributes. The increased awareness and appreciation generated by park visitation can also lead to heightened support for environmental conservation and preservation efforts on a global scale.

National park exploration can have a profound effect on relationships and social bonds. Families and friends who embark on journeys to these natural wonders create lasting memories and share meaningful experiences that strengthen their connections. The shared adventures, the campfire stories, and the challenges overcome together often serve as a source of nostalgia and a bond that endures over time. Many individuals who explore national parks as children go on to introduce their own families to the wonders of these natural sanctuaries, passing down a love for the outdoors from one generation to the next.

In conclusion, exploring national parks has a lasting impact on individuals, communities, and society. These natural sanctuaries inspire a deep appreciation for the environment, foster a passion for learning, and promote mental and physical well-being. They fuel a spirit of adventure and curiosity, stimulate local economies, and contribute to preserving our natural and cultural heritage.

National parks serve as reminders of the beauty and wonder of the natural world and offer a sanctuary where individuals can connect with the Earth and with each other. As these protected areas continue to inspire and enrich the lives of countless visitors, their legacy of conservation, education, and adventure will endure for generations to come.

Planning your next RV adventure

The allure of the open road, the freedom to explore new horizons, and the comfort of having your home on wheels make RV travel an enticing and unforgettable experience. Whether you're a seasoned RV enthusiast or embarking on your first adventure, careful planning is essential to ensure a smooth and enjoyable journey. This section will explore the key steps and considerations involved in planning your next RV adventure, from choosing the right RV to mapping out your route and preparing for the unexpected.

The first and perhaps most crucial step in planning your RV adventure is selecting the right recreational vehicle for your needs and preferences. RVs come in various types, from motorhomes and travel trailers to fifth wheels and pop-up campers, each offering unique features and accommodations. Consider factors such as the size of your travel group, your budget, and your preferred comfort level. Are you looking for a compact camper for solo adventures, a spacious motorhome for family trips, or something in between? Determining your RV type will set the foundation for the rest of your planning.

Once you've chosen your RV, it's essential to familiarize yourself with its operation and maintenance. Understanding how to operate the RV's systems, including plumbing, electrical, and propane, is crucial for a trouble-free journey. Regular maintenance checks, such as inspecting tires, brakes, and fluid levels, should be conducted before hitting the road. If you're new to RVing, consider taking a training course or seeking guidance from experienced RVers to ensure that you're well- prepared for the journey ahead.

The next step is to plan your route and create an itinerary. RV travel offers the flexibility to choose your destinations, and it's essential to balance spontaneity and structure. Research potential stops, national parks, campgrounds, and points of interest along your route. Consider factors such as travel distances, road conditions, and the availability of RV-friendly facilities. Mapping out your itinerary ensures that you make the most of your adventure and helps with campground reservations, which can be essential during peak travel seasons.

Regarding campgrounds, securing accommodations along your route is vital to RV trip planning. Campground options range from state and national parks to private RV parks and campgrounds. Some campgrounds offer full hookups with water, electric, and sewer connections, while others provide more rustic settings with limited amenities. Be sure to research and book your campgrounds well in advance, especially if you plan to visit popular destinations or travel during peak seasons. Some campgrounds may have restrictions or require reservations, so checking their policies and availability is essential.

Packing and provisioning your RV is another crucial aspect of trip planning. Create an essentials checklist, including clothing, kitchen supplies, bedding, and personal items. Keep in mind the storage capacity of your RV and avoid overpacking, as excess weight can affect fuel efficiency and handling. Stock up on groceries and supplies before hitting the road, especially if you plan to travel through remote areas where resources may be limited. A well-organized and adequately stocked RV will ensure that you're prepared for various situations and enjoy a comfortable and convenient journey.

Safety is paramount when planning an RV adventure, and it's essential to equip your RV with the necessary safety gear. Ensure your RV is equipped with smoke detectors, carbon monoxide detectors, and fire extinguishers. Familiarize yourself with the location and operation of these safety devices. Additionally, invest in a quality set of wheel chocks, leveling blocks, and stabilizer jacks to ensure the stability and safety of your RV when parked. Having a comprehensive first-aid kit and knowing how to use it is also crucial for addressing any minor injuries or medical emergencies that may arise.

In addition to safety precautions, it's essential to be prepared for unexpected situations on the road. Develop a contingency plan for breakdowns or mechanical issues, including having contact information for RV repair services and knowing the location of the nearest service centers along your route. Familiarize yourself with the procedures for changing a flat tire, jump-starting the RV, or troubleshooting common RV problems. It's also wise to carry essential tools and spare parts that may be needed for minor repairs.

Weather conditions can significantly impact your RV adventure, so it's essential to monitor weather forecasts and plan accordingly. Extreme weather, such as storms, high winds, or heavy snowfall, can affect road conditions and pose safety risks. Be prepared to alter your travel plans or seek shelter if adverse weather conditions arise. It's also advisable to have an emergency kit that includes essential supplies like blankets, flashlights, non-perishable food, and water in case you encounter unexpected delays or adverse conditions.

Another crucial aspect of RV trip planning is budgeting and financial preparation. Calculate the estimated costs of your journey, including fuel, campground fees, food, entertainment, and miscellaneous expenses. Creating a budget helps you manage your finances while on the road and ensures that you have the necessary funds for your adventure. Be mindful of fuel costs, as RVs are less fuel- efficient than passenger vehicles, and plan your route to minimize unnecessary driving.

Finally, it's essential to consider your environmental impact and practice responsible RVing. Minimize your carbon footprint by conserving water and energy, disposing of waste properly, and following Leave No Trace principles when exploring natural areas. Respect local regulations and guidelines regarding campfires, wildlife interaction, and waste disposal. Being a responsible and eco-conscious RVer preserves the natural beauty of the destinations you visit and sets a positive example for future generations of travelers.

In conclusion, planning your next RV adventure involves a series of thoughtful steps and considerations, from selecting the right RV and familiarizing yourself with its operation to mapping out your route, securing accommodations, and preparing for safety and unexpected situations. By planning and preparing, you can ensure a smooth and enjoyable journey that allows you to make the most of your RV adventure. With careful planning, attention to detail, and a sense of adventure, your next RV trip can be an unforgettable experience that creates lasting memories and enriches your life in countless ways.

Final thoughts and encouragement to continue exploring

The end of an RV trip can be bittersweet. As you return your RV to its storage spot or prepare it for the next adventure, a sense of nostalgia may wash over you. The memories of picturesque landscapes, campfire conversations, and the freedom of the open road linger, leaving you with a yearning for more. In this section, we'll explore the feelings that often accompany the conclusion of an RV trip and offer words of encouragement to continue exploring and embracing the RV lifestyle.

It's entirely normal to experience a mix of emotions as your RV trip ends. The familiarity of your home-on-wheels becomes comforting, and the thought of parting with it can be somewhat melancholic. Yet, the experiences you've gained, the places you've seen, and the memories you've created are precious treasures that remain with you long after the journey concludes. These memories are not meant to fade away but to serve as a source of inspiration and motivation for future adventures.

One of the beautiful aspects of the RV lifestyle is that there are always more destinations to discover, new roads to explore, and hidden gems to unearth. The vast and diverse world offers an endless array of landscapes, cultures, and experiences to explore. The end of one RV trip merely marks the beginning of planning the next. Let your curiosity guide you as you dream of the places you'd like to visit, the scenic routes you'd like to traverse, and the adventures you'd like to embark upon.

The people you meet on the road, both fellow RV travelers and locals, often leave a lasting impact. The shared stories, campfire conversations, and the kindness of strangers can enrich your journey in unexpected ways. The connections forged during your RV adventure can remind you of the human connections that transcend geographical boundaries. Cherish these relationships, and know that as you continue exploring, you'll have the opportunity to meet new friends and create new bonds that add depth and meaning to your adventures.

While the memories of your RV trip are invaluable, it's essential to remember that the RV lifestyle isn't confined to a single journey. It's a way of life that offers a sense of freedom, a thirst for exploration, and a connection to the natural world that can be sustained long-term. You don't have to wait for the next extended road trip to enjoy the benefits of RV living. Consider weekend getaways, short vacations, or even day trips to nearby parks or attractions. These smaller adventures can keep the spirit of exploration alive and provide opportunities for relaxation and rejuvenation.

Moreover, the lessons learned during your RV trip, such as self-sufficiency, adaptability, and resourcefulness, can be applied to other aspects of your life. The RV lifestyle often encourages a minimalist mindset and a focus on experiences over possessions. Use these principles to simplify and enhance your everyday life, reducing stress and focusing on what truly matters. The RV lifestyle can inspire you to live with intention, savor the present moment, and prioritize pursuing your passions and dreams.

Additionally, consider ways to give back to the communities you encounter during your RV travels. Whether through volunteer work, supporting local businesses, or contributing to environmental conservation efforts, your RV journey can positively impact the places you visit. Engaging in acts of kindness and responsible travel practices enriches your experiences and helps preserve the beauty and authenticity of the destinations you explore.

The end of an RV trip doesn't mean the end of adventure. Rather, it begins a new chapter filled with anticipation, curiosity, and a sense of wanderlust. The RV lifestyle is a journey that extends beyond the miles traveled and the destinations visited. It's a mindset that encourages a lifelong love of exploration and an appreciation for the world's wonders, both great and small.

In conclusion, as you conclude your RV trip and prepare for the next stage of your journey, remember that the experiences, friendships, and lessons learned along the way are the true treasures of the RV lifestyle. Embrace the sense of nostalgia and use it as a source of motivation to continue exploring, whether it's near or far. The world is your oyster, and the RV lifestyle is your ticket to a lifetime of adventure, self-discovery, and connection with the beauty of our planet. So, as you bid farewell to one journey, let it be a prelude to countless more, and may your RV adventures continue to enrich your life in ways you've yet to imagine.

CONCLUSION

In the book "Park and Play: Discovering National Parks from the Comfort of Your RV," we have embarked on an extraordinary journey through the beautiful landscapes and diverse cultural treasures that the National Park Service of the United States of America offers. Those individuals who are looking for the experience of a lifetime while staying in the comfort of their recreational vehicles have found this book to be a guide, an inspiration, and a companion.

As we come to the end of this journey, it is essential to keep in mind that the beauty of traveling in an RV lies not only in the places we visit but also in the experiences, connections, and memories that we create along the way. We are invited by the national parks to become stewards of these priceless places, which are more than just scenic wonders; they are the living embodiment of our nation's natural and historical heritage, and they invite us to become stewards of these places.

The book "Park and Play" has provided not only information about the history, significance, and management of national parks but also advice on how to choose an RV, how to budget your money, and travel tips. All readers, whether they are seasoned RV enthusiasts or newcomers to the world of RV travel, have been given the ability to embark on their own adventures as a result of this book.

In the end, "Park and Play" celebrates the joy of exploration, the wonder of the great outdoors, and the spirit of adventure that never goes out of style. This book is intended to serve as your reliable companion as you prepare to embark on your RV journey to discover the national parks. It will lead you to the wonders that are waiting for you within the pristine landscapes, rich history, and vibrant culture of America's national treasures. Now is the time to start your engines, get out on the open road, and allow the experiences you have within our national parks to serve as your motivation for a lifetime of exploration and appreciation of the world that surrounds humanity.

Thank you for buying and reading/ listening to our book. If you found this book useful/ helpful please take a few minutes and leave a review on the platform where you purchased our book. Your feedback matters greatly to us.

9 798869 123077